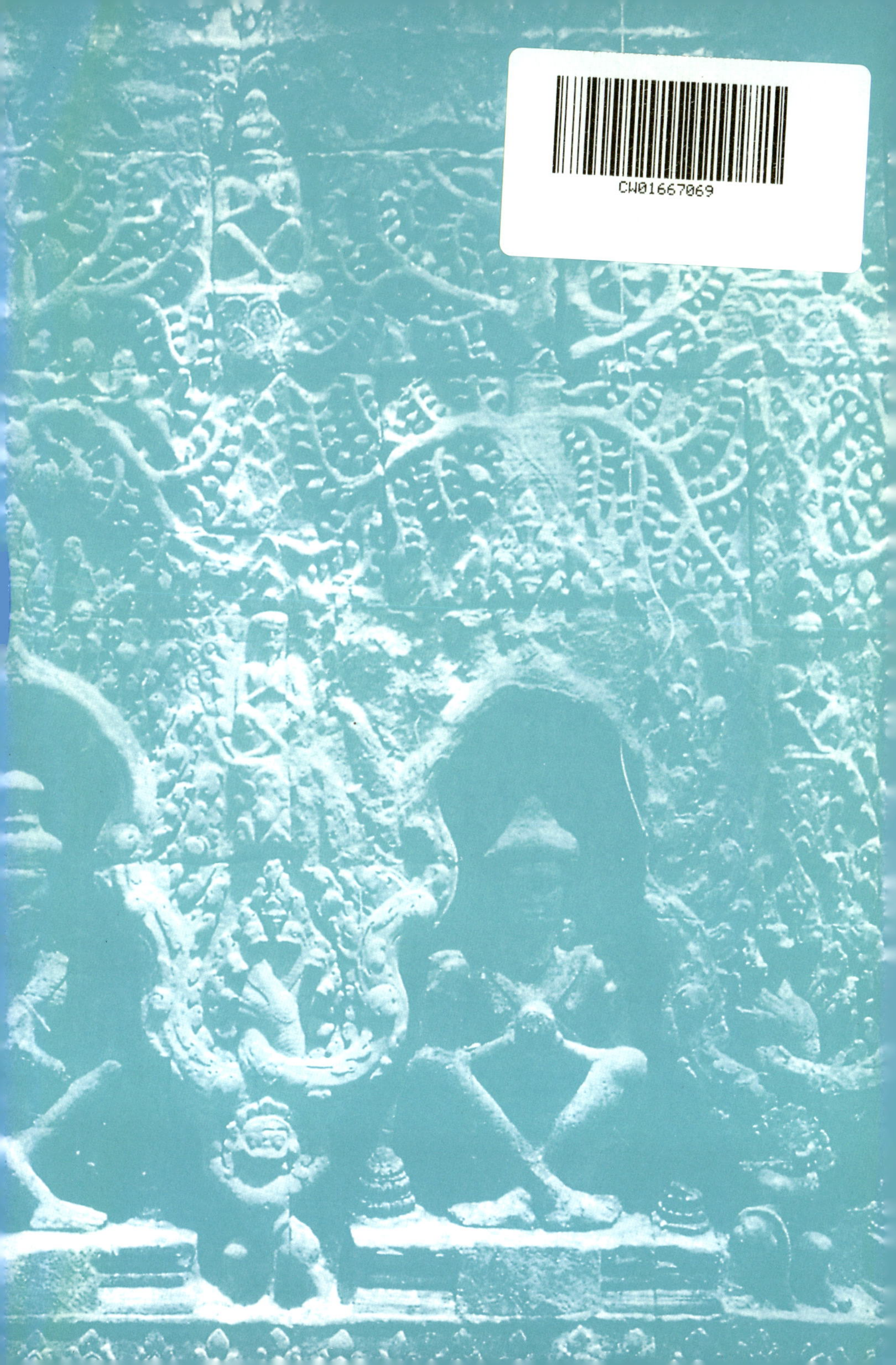

A PILGRIMAGE TO ANGKOR

PIERRE LOTI
(JULIEN VIAUD)

A PILGRIMAGE TO ANGKOR

BASED ON A TRANSLATION BY

W. P. BAINES

EDITED AND INTRODUCED BY

MICHAEL SMITHIES

WITH ILLUSTRATIONS BY

EUAYPORN KERDCHOUAY

SILKWORM BOOKS

OTHER BOOKS BY THE EDITOR

Old Bangkok
Descriptions of Old Siam
Abbé de Choisy, Journal of a Voyage to Siam in 1685 and 1686
The Siamese Embassy to the Sun King: The Personal Memoirs of Kosa Pan
The Discourses at Versailles of the First Siamese Ambassadors to France 1686–7
A Busy Week: Tales from Today's Thailand
Bight of Bangkok
A Thai Boyhood
A Singapore Boyhood
A Javanese Boyhood
Yogyakarta, Cultural Heart of Indonesia
Discovering Thailand (with Achille Clarac)
The Cultural Sites of Burma, Thailand, and Cambodia
(with Jacques Dumarçay)
The Cultural Sites of Malaysia, Singapore, and Indonesia
(with Jacques Dumarçay)
The Siamese Memoir of Count Claude de Forbin 1685–1688
Alexander Hamilton: A Scottish Sea Captain in Southeast Asia 1689–1723
Chaumont and Choisy: Aspects of the Embassy to Siam 1685
A Resounding Failure: Martin and the French in Siam 1672–1693

First published in 1996 by
Silkworm Books
54/1 Sridonchai Road, Chiang Mai 50100, Thailand.
Second imprint (corrected) 1999

ISBN 974-7100-82-7

Design by T. Jittidejarak
Set in 11 pt. Garamond by Silk Type

Printed in Thailand by O.S. Printing House, Bangkok.

CONTENTS

Chapter headings have been added by the editor.

ILLUSTRATIONS

All illustrations have been provided by Euayporn Kerdchouay, except for the last two.

PREFACE

IT is many years since Loti's book on Angkor has been available in English; the ending of copyright on his works has led to the reappearance in French of three editions since 1989, one in the omnibus edition of his travel accounts edited by Claude Martin (Paris, Laffont, 1991), to which the present publication is indebted for some of the material found in the introduction and notes.

Loti's fulsome, often romantic prose may not be to the taste of everyone, but he has the ability to capture in words the essence of the feeling for a place. The jungle-covered temples of Angkor perfectly suited his mood and his pen. Others may present the hard facts concerning the complex better, but few equal Loti's evocative power.

In making this work available again to the English-reading public, I should like to thank Dr Henry Ginsburg, of the Oriental and India Office Collections, British Library, Madame Lucienne Girard, of Coulon, France, and most particularly Khun Euayporn Kerdchouay at the Siam Society, for making available some of his slides of Angkor taken in recent years.

For too long, internal conflicts have placed the Angkor complex out of bounds to visitors. Now that most of the temples can be seen again, Loti's work can once more inspire travellers to this unequalled archaeological site which bears witness to the greatness of Cambodia's past.

Michael Smithies
Bua Yai, October 1995

INTRODUCTION

PIERRE LOTI (1850–1923), a member of the Académie Française from 1891 when he became its then youngest member, was a curious person and a writer with a mixed reputation which is currently rising.

He was born Louis Marie Julien Viaud in the naval station of Rochefort in southwest France, in a family house in the Rue de Fleurus, now the Rue Pierre Loti. Julien was the third child of the Catholic Théodore Viaud, born 1804, and the Protestant Nadine Texier, born 1810; his father was chief secretary to the Rochefort town hall, a poet and dramatist in his youth, and the author, with E.J. Fleury, city librarian, of a history of the town and port of Rochefort. As a boy, Julien frequently went to the nearby island of Oléron to spend holidays there accompanied by his brother, Gustave (born 1838), and sister, Marie (born 1831), with his mother's relatives.

Gustave Viaud left in 1859 for Tahiti as naval surgeon, returning to Rochefort in 1862 before leaving for duty in Cochin-China. His younger brother Julien decided to enter the navy at this time; having until then had a private education, he was enrolled in the Collège de Rochefort, where he was an indifferent student; under his sister's influence, he learnt to play the piano. His sister married a local tax-collector in 1864, and the following year his revered elder brother died at sea of dysentery while returning from Saigon.

The year 1866 was even blacker. His father, now municipal tax collector, was accused of theft, and spent some days in prison. He was freed on bail, and two years later declared innocent, but lost his position, having to take up a minor post in a bank; worse, he was required by the court to reimburse in full the value of the missing securities, which were never found. Julien failed the entrance examination for the naval college, and left for Paris, where he began to write his Intimate Journal which he kept up for most of his life.

In 1867 however he passed the competitive entrance examination for the Ecole Navale and went to Brest for studies on board the training ship *Borda*, passing out in August 1869 as midshipman, and beginning to sail the seven seas. He was in New York the following year when he learned of the death of his father, and saw service in the North and Baltic seas during the Franco-Prussian war. He started to travel widely as part of his career, going to Senegal, Brazil, Chile, Tahiti, California and Haiti in 1871–2. His income allowed him to purchase from his mother the family house in Rochefort in 1871. He was to add to this the two neighbouring houses, giving him some thirty rooms which he transformed into a personal museum, complete with a mediaeval hall, a Renaissance Spanish dining room, Turkish and Arab rooms, a Japanese pagoda, and even a mosque, while leaving the original family rooms as they were: this extraordinary ensemble was opened as a municipal museum in 1969.

His first published work came out in 1872, in the form of three articles on Easter Island published in *L'Illustration*, illustrated with his own drawings. A stay in Tahiti gave him material for his *Marriage of Loti*, and a period in Senegal in 1873 that for the *Novel of a Spahi*. The following year saw the first of his much-publicized amorous affairs with exotic ladies, this particular one being an unknown person from Senegal. The bravado with which these were announced to the world, and the discretion over details, gave a public facade to his less conventional private activities.

Loti always had to prove himself; he was small of stature and tried to make up for this. During leave in 1875 he took a course at a gymnastic school and the following year appeared on several occasions as a clown and acrobat in the Etruscan Circus in Toulon. After that he was in Constantinople (Istanbul) where another much-publicized affair took place, that of Aziyadé. In complete antithesis, he went on a Trappist retreat in 1878 which gave him "a detachment from life", though a second stay the following year left him disillusioned. His romance *Aziyadé* appeared in 1879, without any author's name, with Calman-Lévy (who was to remain his publisher throughout his life); it met with no success, unlike his second volume, *Le Mariage de Loti* (1880), which appeared in serial form the previous year, edited by Juliette Adam, a literary patroness, friend of Alphonse Daudet among others, who introduced Loti into the world of letters. From this time on, all his writings were under his pen name acquired in Tahiti in 1872.

He was promoted in the ranks of the navy, retained his links with Rochefort (he occupied the post of secretary to its elected council for a year), and continued to travel widely as part of his naval duties. In 1883 he signed, as Pierre Loti, an article published in *Le Figaro* relating the civilian massacres in the attack on Hué, which caused his recall. By the time he arrived in Paris it was found he had exaggerated nothing, and the matter was dropped. But it caused him to wonder what he would do if he had to choose between his naval career and his literary one, and he had already decided in favour of the former.

After more Far Eastern service in 1885, in China and Japan, he returned to Rochefort in 1886, where he was to stay on duty until 1890. An aunt, doubtless thinking her thirty-six year old nephew a little late in marrying, produced Blanche Franc de Ferrière, nine years younger than Loti, of old Protestant Bordeaux and Dordogne stock. They were married in October and spent their honeymoon in Spain; a son was born prematurely the following year, and died.

Loti the writer was recognized publicly in 1887 with the award of the Legion of Honour (as chevalier, the lowest rank), and he spent some time in Romania at the invitation of its literary Queen Elisabeth. His oriental novel *Madame Chrysanthème* was published, with great success. His income was now sufficient for him to begin to indulge in his great extravaganzas, which must have astonished the burgers of conservative Rochefort: in 1888 he threw a fancy-dress 'Louis XI party' attended by many luminaries of Parisian society; the visit of his old friend Sarah Bernhardt to his exotic home (already complete with Turkish and Arab rooms and Japanese pagoda) when acting in Rochefort must have caused tongues to wag even more.

The Louis XI masquerade was followed the next year by an Arab party, after the birth of his son Samuel (who lived until 1969) and having been one of the party escorting the new French minister in Morocco presenting his letters of credence to the sultan. The account of that journey appeared in print the following year, when Loti made his first attempt to enter the Académie Française, which was unsuccessful. His childhood memoirs were published then, and he made another visit to Constantinople, where he was received by the sultan.

His second attempt to enter the Academy in 1891 succeeded (he won with eighteen votes, against ten for his nearest rival, Henri de Bornier, and none, in the final vote, for the eminent naturalist novelist Zola). Two of his novels were turned into plays and staged in 1893, and he met the twenty-seven year old Spanish Basque Crucita Gainza, whom he installed, after a trip to the Holy Lands in 1894 in the company of "the handsome Léo", the young sailor Léopold Thémèze, in a house in Rochefort which he visited almost every day, while his wife continued to live in the family house. The good burgers must have been still more astonished at the activities of the naval commander who had just completed three years working in the maritime prefecture there.

A son was born of his mistress in 1895 (another followed two years later), and in 1896 Loti's mother died, aged ninety-six. These domestic upheavals were, in 1898, matched by one that convulsed France, the Dreyfus affair; Loti, as a good officer, at first believed Dreyfus guilty, was shaken by the subsequent revelations, but tried to avoid taking any public position. He was retired the same year from the navy (along with twenty-seven others) in a move by the Secretary of State for the Navy to renew the senior ranks, and promoted to be officer of the Legion of Honour. But the State Council reversed the ministerial decision, and Loti was reintegrated into naval service, though without being given a specific position, and without pay, being placed at the disposition of the Ministry of Foreign Affairs. He took advantage of this to go to Persia and India, accompanied by the young Edmond Gueffier, like Viaud from the Charente region, who was doing his military service on board Viaud's ship, the *Javelot*, from 1896–7; the excuse for the journey was the presentation of the Palmes Académiques to the Maharajah of Travancore.

Loti was reinstated in active service in 1900, and joined Vice-Admiral Pottier as aide-de-camp on a journey to China, as part of the western response to the Boxer uprising. He went from China to Japan and Korea, and at the end of 1901, during a shore stay in Saigon from 23 November to 5 December, he made his journey to Angkor, of which more below.

He returned to France in 1902 and was given the post of aide-de-camp to the naval prefect of Rochefort. His taste for high living and dressing up had not abated; on completion of the Chinese room the following year, he threw a grand Chinese party. Publications continued; he even produced, in collaboration with Emile Vedel in 1904, a translation of *King Lear*. He was further promoted in 1906 to ship's captain, then travelled in Egypt. But by 1909 his wife Blanche had had enough of Rochefort and her equivocal position there; she retired to the Dordogne where she died in 1940. Loti celebrated by going to London and being received by Queen Alexandra.

Loti was put on reserve on reaching the age of sixty in 1910, promoted commander of the Legion of Honour, and travelled once more to Istanbul. In 1912 his *Pilgrimage to Angkor* was published and he travelled to the United States, which he did not like, and where he was received by President Taft. The Turkish cause continued to occupy him; he published articles in its favour and went once more to Istanbul in 1913.

At the outbreak of the World War, at his request Loti was mobilized, but sent home. The military governor of Paris allowed him to go to the front and make reports. Against the wishes of the Secretariat of State for the Navy, he was given an active post in the supreme command of the military governor in Paris. His attempt to take part in the defence of Verdun was rebuffed by Pétain: "I have no need of sailors to defend Verdun." He nevertheless took part in several reconnaissance missions. On leaves, he continued to meet the great and noble: Albert I of Belgium, Victor-Emmanuel II of Italy, Alphonso XIII of Spain. He was demobilized early in 1918 but managed to join the army in the north; when the German offensive increased, he was ordered to withdraw. The chief of staff told the sixty-eight year old writer and naval officer, "I consider you have passed the limit of your strength". He was compensated with the award of the Croix de Guerre, with citation.

But he was ageing and in preparation for his death he stopped writing his daily journal; the following year he was taken off the reserve list as being over age. His son Samuel married in 1920 a daughter of a former marine prefect of Rochefort (the witnesses were the President of the Republic, Poincaré, and Lacaze, former Secretary of State for the Navy). He was partially paralyzed in 1921 and gave up writing. In 1923 he left Rochefort to spend a few days in Hendaye, in the cottage he had bought years before. He died there on 10 June, his body was brought back to

Rochefort and laid out in the Renaissance room, and a state funeral took place on 16 June (with no representative from the Académie Française). He was buried, at his request, in Saint Pierre on Oléron.

* * *

Loti, as his text makes clear, had always wanted to see Angkor. He kept his own personal museum, in which, among his brother's papers, he came across a description of Angkor which fascinated him. After serving in Peking, he left on the *Redoutable* from Nagasaki in October 1901 for France, which he did not reach until April the following year. Between 1883 and 1885, on four different ships, he had called at Saigon, but had never been able to realize his dream of seeing the ancient Cambodian capital. This time his cruiser stayed from 5 November 1901 to 14 March 1902 in Indo-China, and Loti was quick to seek permission to take two weeks' leave to visit Angkor.

Accompanied by his servant Osman Daney (who, in spite of his name, which was given him by his grandfather in memory of a good Turkish friend met in the Crimean War, was pure Gascon), he took the train to My Tho, went by steamer upriver to Phnom Penh, where he stayed two nights and saw the royal palace, and resumed his journey to the entrance to the Tonle Sap lake. There he transferred to big covered sampans and late at night landed in what was then Siamese territory. Buffalo carts took his party to the town of Siem Reap, where he arrived about midday on 28 November. He left on 30 November, likewise taking five days to return, using the same means of transport, except that elephants were put at his disposition by King Norodom of Cambodia to visit a royal mausoleum close to the village of Kampong Luong.

Thus he stayed less than two days in Angkor, as his personal diaries, his *Journal Intime*, make clear. He obviously thought this rather short, and added to his printed account of his journey a full day, that of 30 November (which in fact was spent travelling from eight in the morning, not, as he makes out, exploring Angkor Thom and the Bayon again and leaving in the early evening). In reality, he arrived in Phnom Penh late on 1 December, and left at midnight the next day to arrive in Saigon on 3 December in time to sup on board his ship.

He was not able, therefore, to describe in great detail the whole site of Angkor, nor did he intend to. This is, as the French title makes clear, a pilgrimage to Angkor; he was fulfilling a desire of his youth. While the description of Angkor Wat and the Bayon is the central part of the text, it is framed by the journey to and from the site, and by the first and last (the thirteenth) chapters which go back and forwards in time. When Loti wrote up his text, adding material gleaned in the intervening years, he was already sixty; the signs of age, of reflection, are clear in his writing. But what remains in the reader's mind are his vivid descriptions of the temples, their crowded reliefs, the jungle invading everything, the relative peace of the Buddhist temple at the foot of Angkor Wat, the reception given him in the palace in Phnom Penh with the ailing king (who was to die in 1904) symbolically represented by his emblems of power.

The text was published by Calmann-Lévy in February 1912, more than a year after being completed by Loti. Four extracts appeared in *L'Illustration* between 16 December 1911 and 6 January 1912. The English translation appeared, rather quaintly, with the title *Siam* under the imprint of T. Werner Laurie, of London, but with no date of publication. This was, according to the British Library, first published in 1913, and again in 1929. Not long after Loti's death in 1923 his reputation suffered a fairly swift decline, and no further editions in English of his text on Angkor are known to have have appeared. Recently, however, there has been a revival of interest in his writings, particularly in France, fuelled in part by his works coming out of copyright, and in part by the increasing accessibility of the more remote places he visited.

Yet Loti's work remains immensely readable, and has the eternal appeal of the exotic. His novels, from *Pecheur d'Islande* (*Icelandic Fisherman*), his greatest success, through his Turkish and other 'oriental' works, are still sold and read. His travel writing was in a class of its own, impressionistic, possibly even journalistic (of a very superior kind); his reporting on Peking after the Boxer uprising, which was published in 1902 at *Les Derniers Jours de Pékin* (*The Last Days of Peking*) is marvellously evocative and very detailed.

Though not long enough in Angkor to add to his extraordinary collection of memorabilia in Rochefort (in 1886 he brought back six hundred kilograms of souvenirs from his trip to Japan), and therefore, unlike Malraux in the 1920s, able to have a clear conscience in respect of the monuments he visited, he came back with something more vital: the impression of magnificent constructions lost in time, surrounded by the tropical forest. These are his legacy, which is that of Angkor too.

* * *

The original English translator of Loti's text on Angkor was F.W. Baines, who also translated his *Tale of the Pyranees (Ramuntcho), A Tale of Brittany (Mon frère Yves), Morocco (Au Maroc), Egypt (La Mort de Philae)*, and *Jerusalem*. In the Angkor text, Baines, perhaps working against time (it was produced within a year of the appearance of the original French edition), allowed himself, at times, some freedom with the original, and introduced some errors. In the first chapter, for example, he speaks of 'palms' instead of banyans, 'tasks' instead of homework, 'scholar' instead of schoolboy, 'barbaric' instead of Oceanic; he omits an important adjective qualifying the ruins, adds a phrase of his own, and gets a tense wrong, altering the meaning of the original.

Nevertheless, Baines on the whole appears to have kept much of the flavour of the original, even if his version is sometimes excessively poeticized by the introduction of archaic terms and inverted constructions. Consequently this edition has used Baines' translation as its base, but changed it where it is needlessly unfaithful to the French original: thus 'grim warship' in chapter II becomes, as it should be, 'heavy battleship' and the added phrase about Saigon 'After an acquaintance of many years' has been eliminated. *Brousse* throughout has been rendered by jungle when near Angkor and undergrowth elsewhere, not by 'bush', in conformity with the natural landscape of the areas Loti passes through; 'pagoda' has been replaced by temple, 'idol' by statue, and so on. All the 'hithers' and 'yonders' and other archaisms of the original translation have been removed, and three serious slips corrected. The final result, it is hoped, is less fanciful and more faithful to the original.

* * * * *

SIAM

BY

PIERRE LOTI

TRANSLATED FROM THE FRENCH BY

W.P. BAINES AND MICHAEL SMITHIES

ILLUSTRATIONS BY

EUAYPORN KERDCHOUAY
MICHAEL SMITHIES

AUTHOR'S DEDICATION
to Monsieur Paul Doumer[1]

DEAR FRIEND,

You were governing with such admirable talents—when I was there last. I owe it to your charming hospitality that I was able in a few short days to penetrate as far as Angkor. May I ask, then, that you will accept the dedication of this narrative, as a token of my affectionate gratitude, and also of my admiration?

And will you forgive me for having said that our Empire in Indo-China would lack grandeur and, more especially, would lack stability—you who have worked so gloriously and so peacefully to ensure it will last? What can I say: I do not believe in the future of our distant colonial conquests. And I mourn the thousands and thousands of our brave young soldiers, who, before your arrival, we laid in those Asiatic cemeteries, when we might so well have spared their precious lives, and risked them only in the last defence of our beloved homeland.

Pierre Loti

1. Paul Doumer (1857–1932) became president of the Senate in 1927 and president of the Republic in 1931, to be assassinated the following year. He was governor-general of Indo-China from 1897 to 1902, during which time he put the colony on a sound administrative footing and undertook public works. He cared little for local reaction; the peoples of Indo-China complained of excessive centralization, and heavy taxation, among other things.

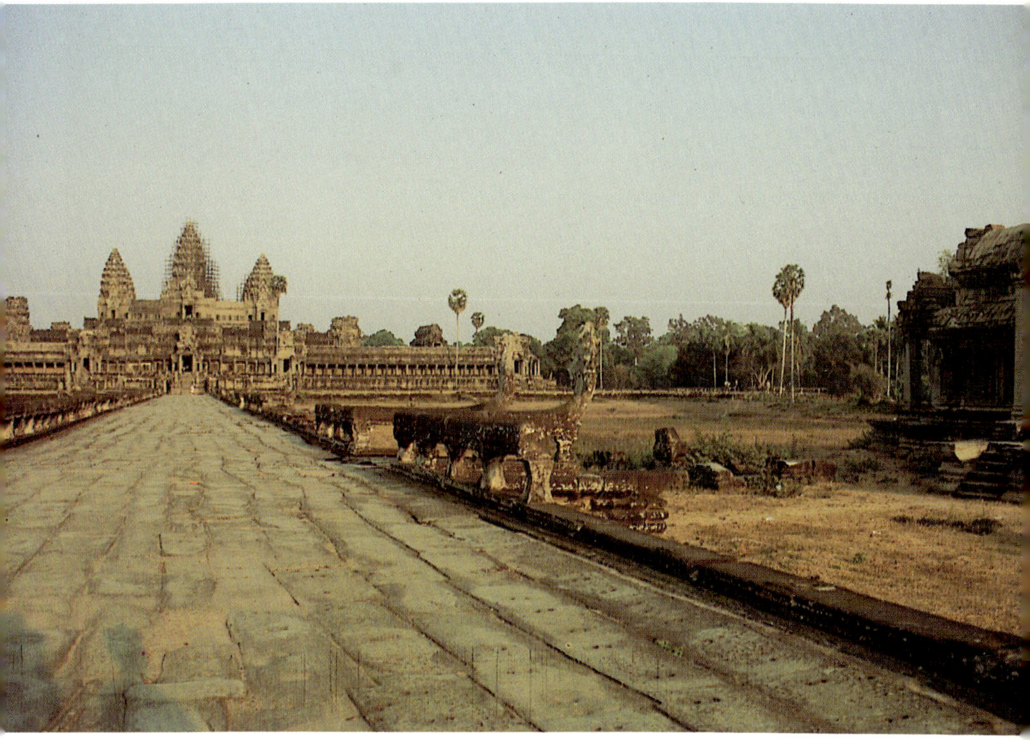

1. Angkor Wat (Suryavarman II, first half of twelfth century): inner approach causeway

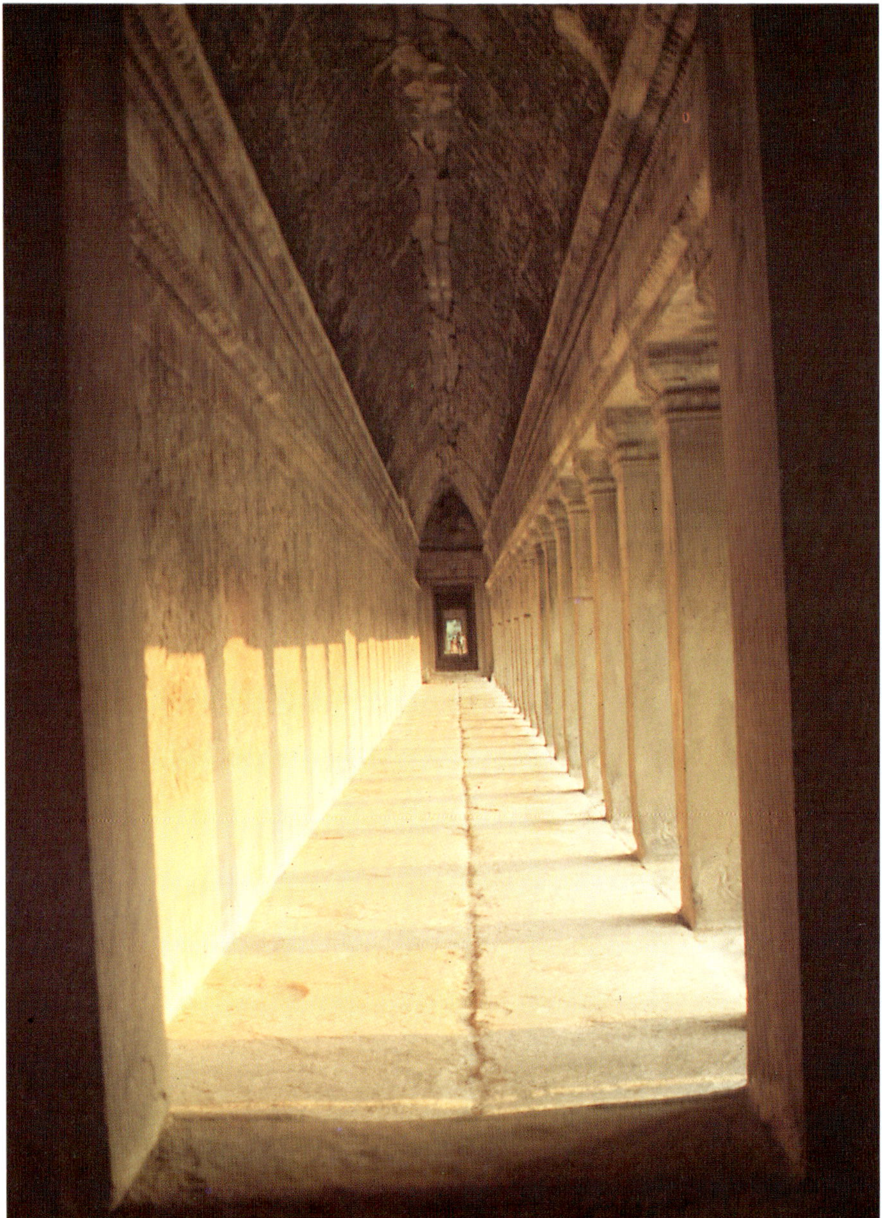

2. Angkor Wat: outer gallery by bas-reliefs

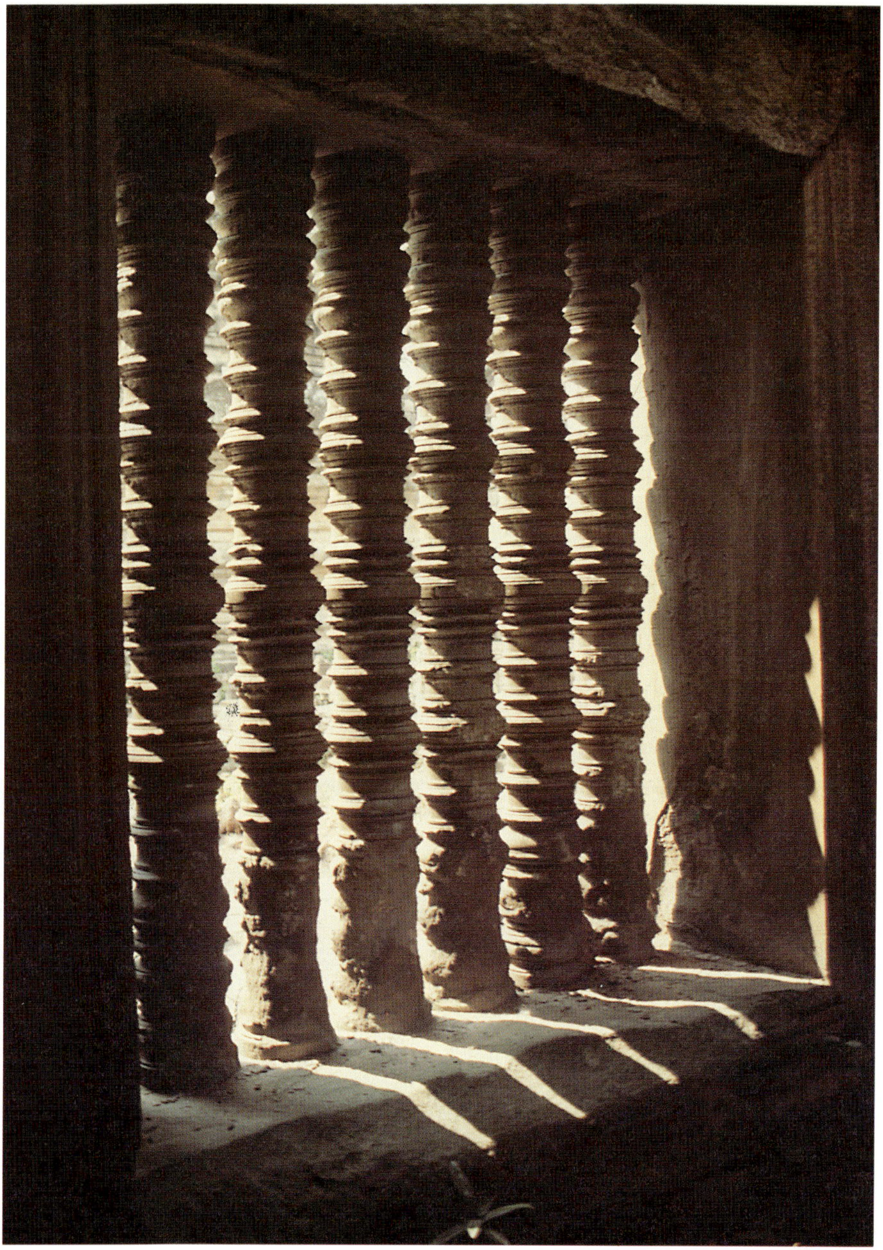

3. Angkor Wat: baluster window

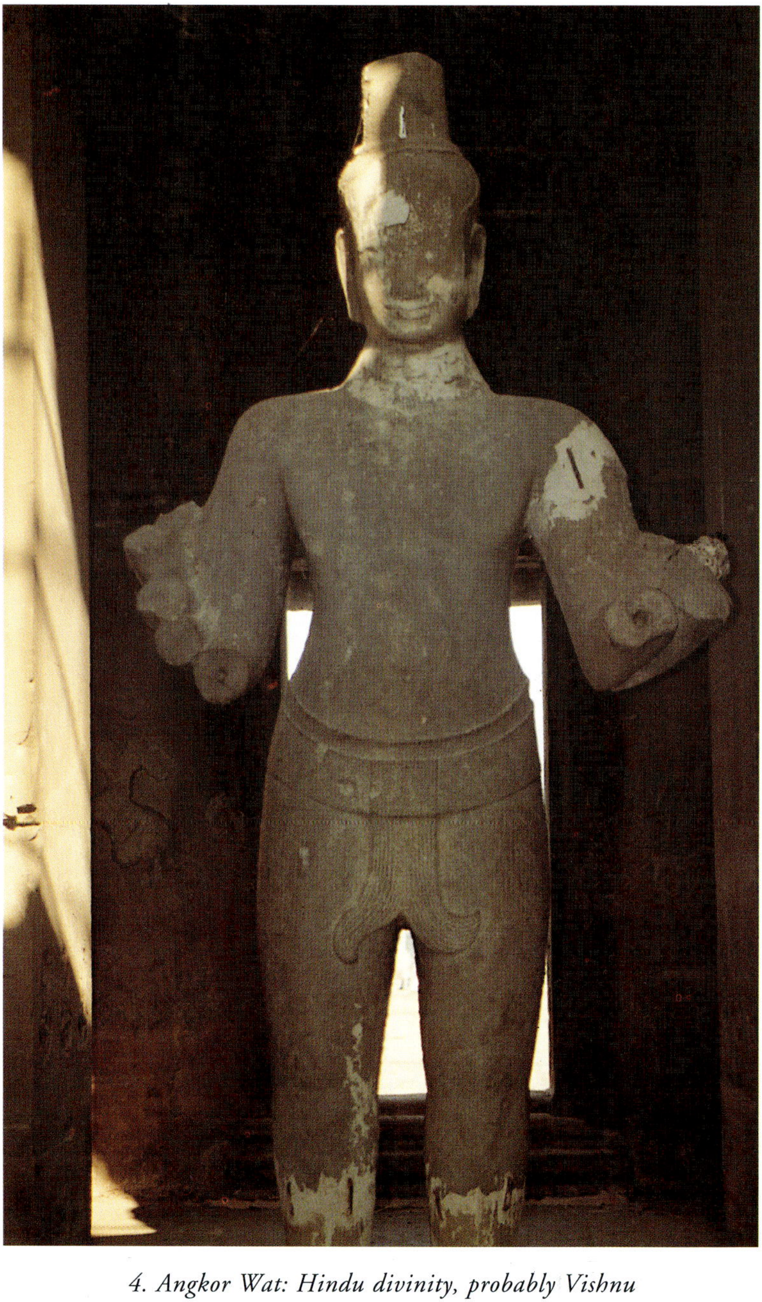

4. Angkor Wat: Hindu divinity, probably Vishnu

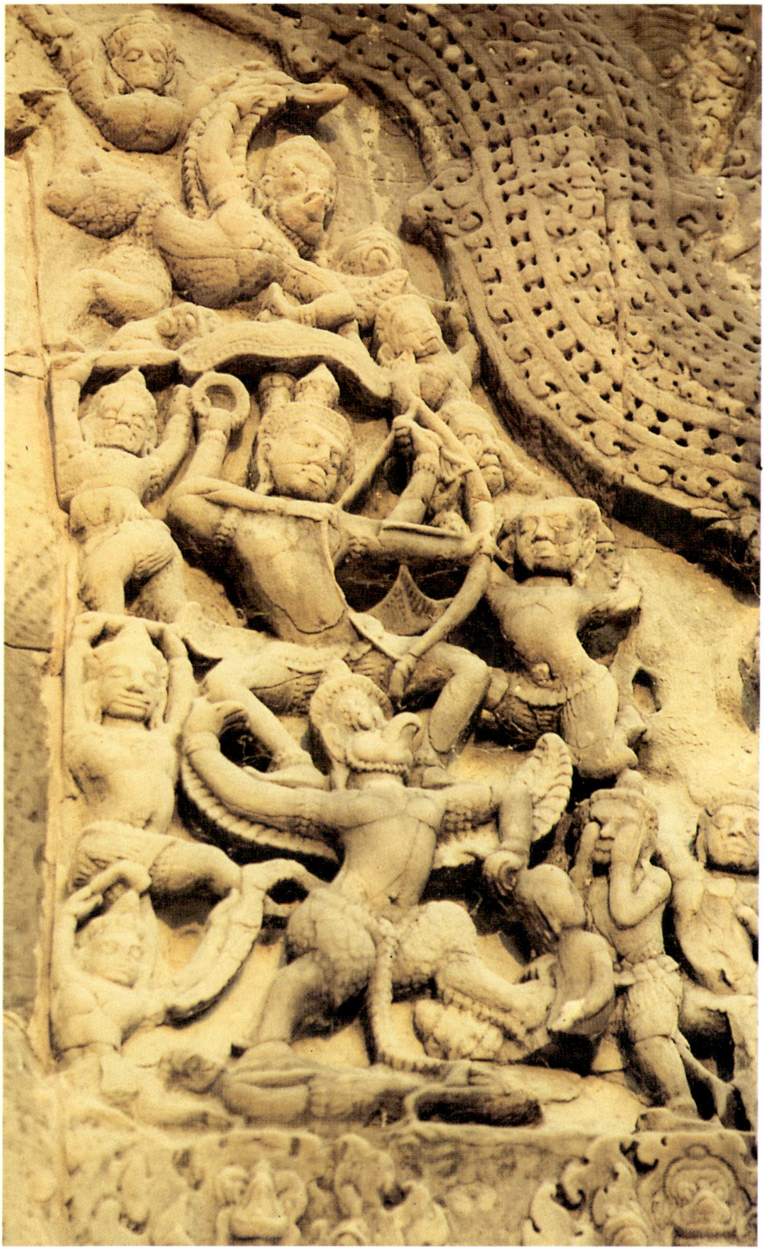

5. Angkor Wat: detail of bas-relief

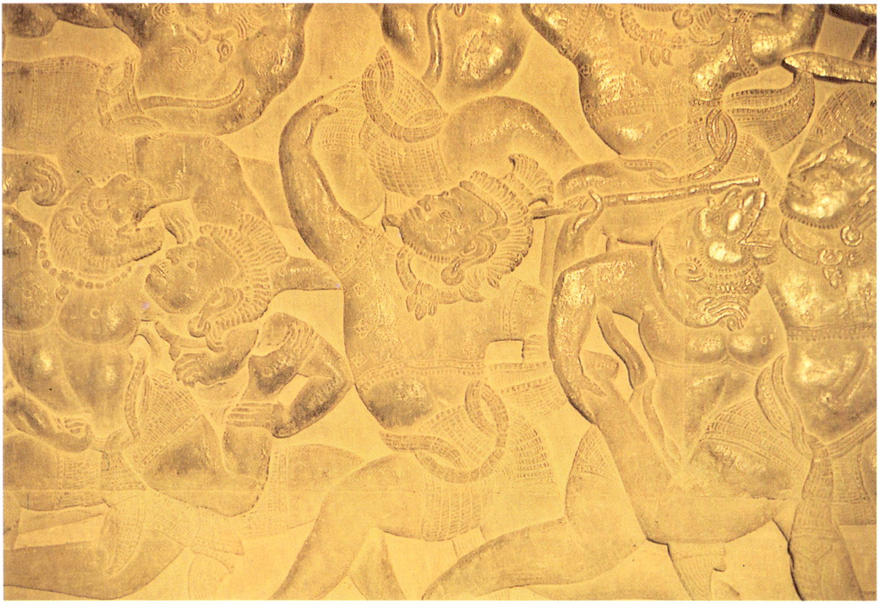

6. Angkor Wat: detail of bas-relief

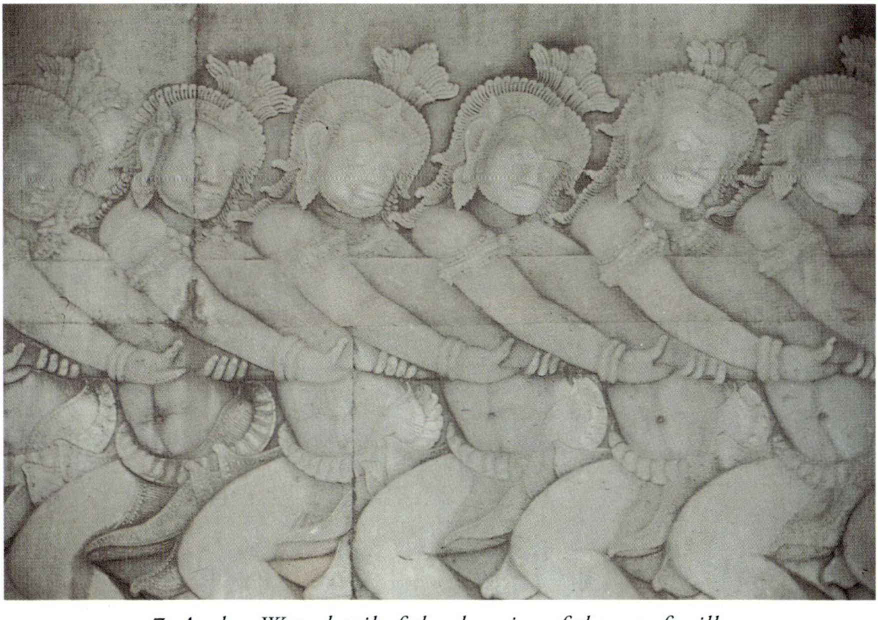

7. Angkor Wat: detail of the churning of the sea of milk

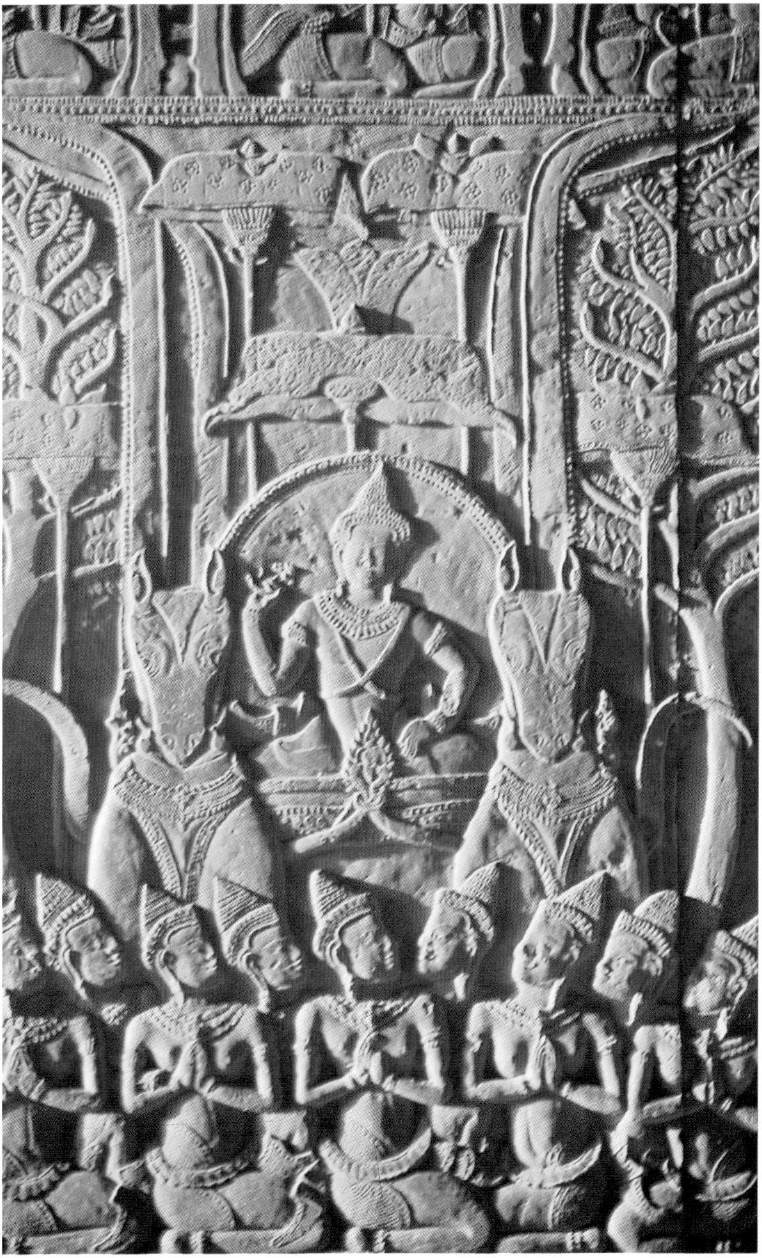

8. *Angkor Wat: Suryavarman II in state*

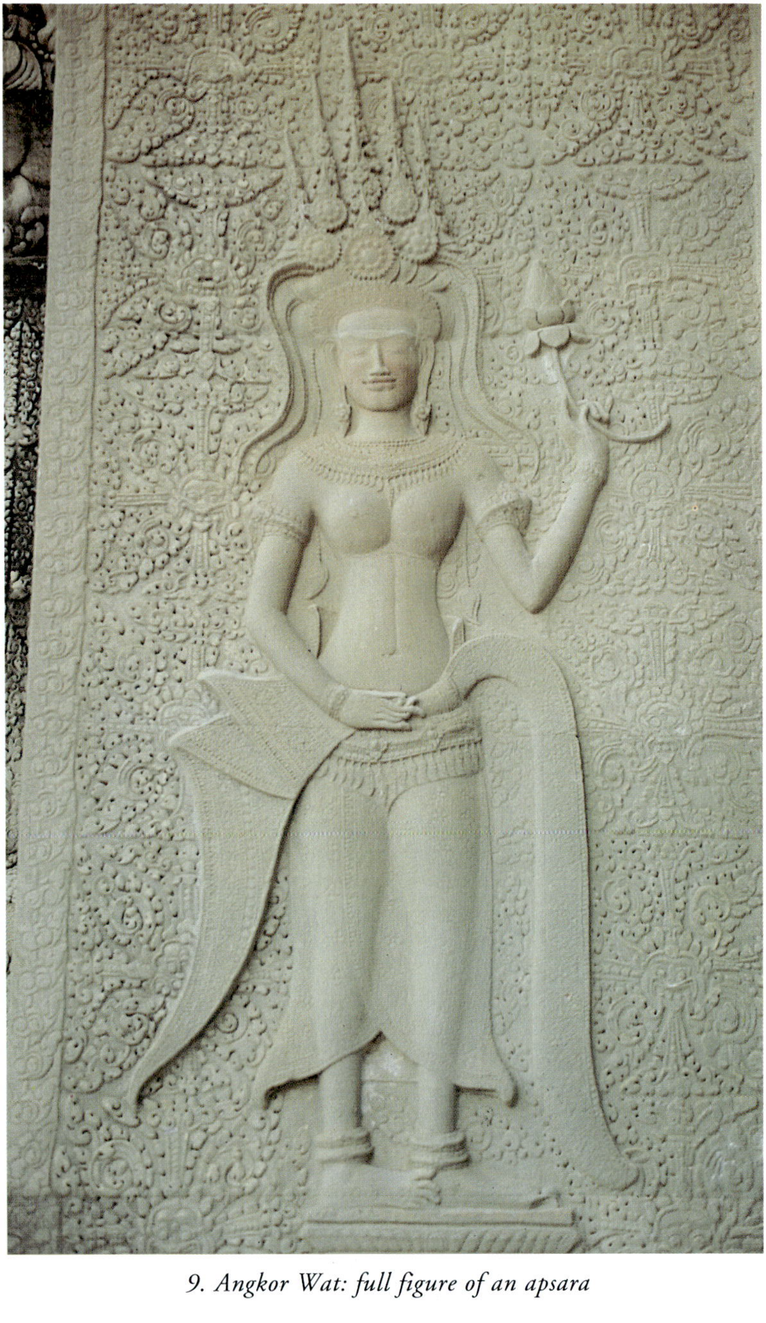

9. Angkor Wat: full figure of an apsara

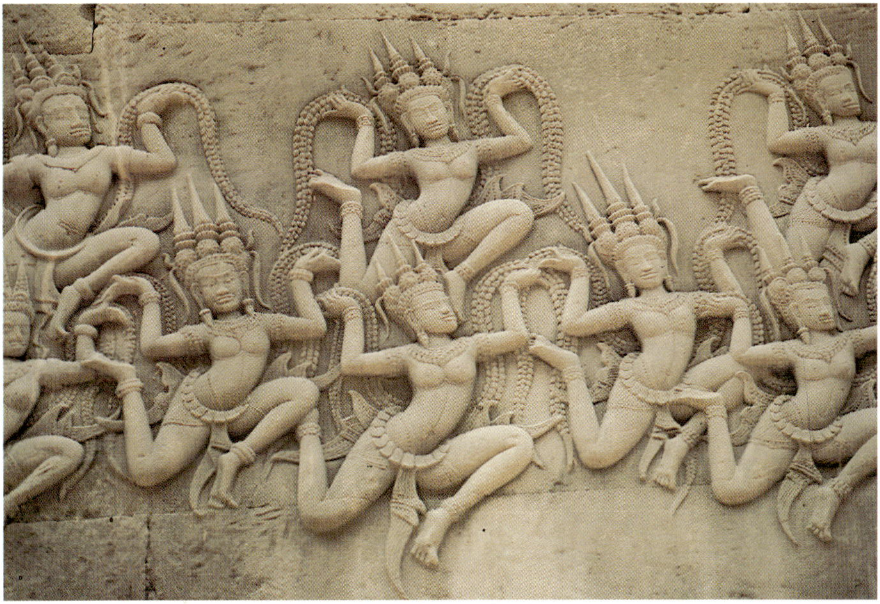

10. *Angkor Wat: flight of apsara*

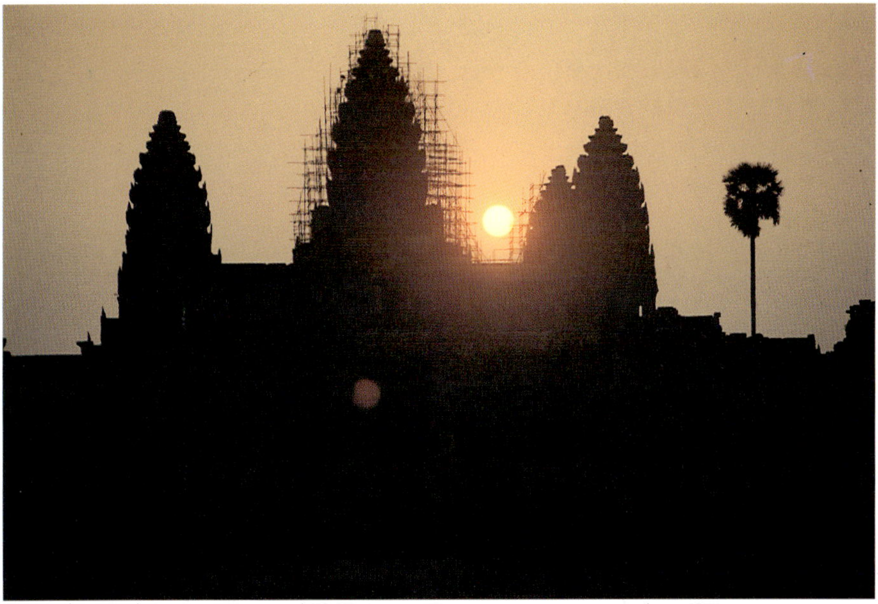

11. *Angkor Wat: the central shrine, viewed late afternoon from the rear*

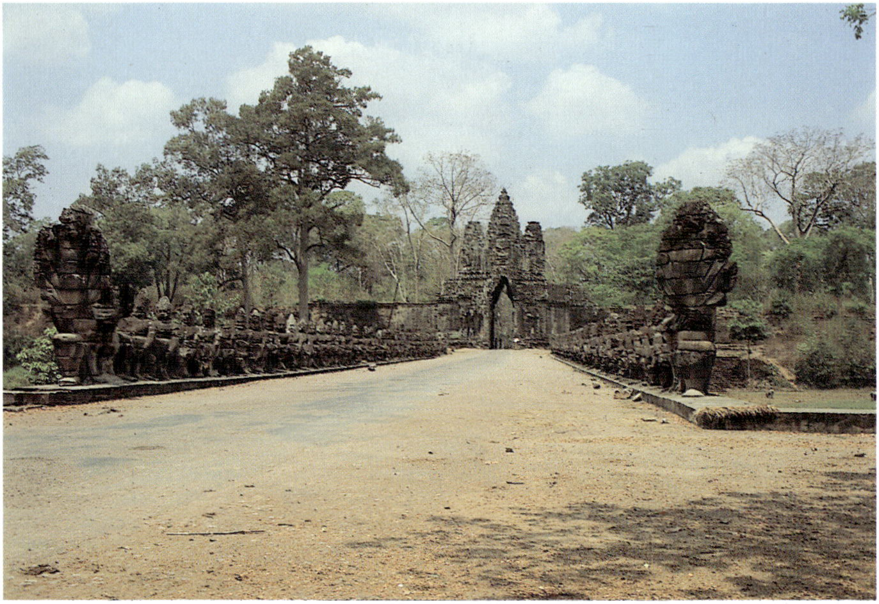

12. Angkor Thom (Jayavarman VII, late twelfth century): the southern gateway

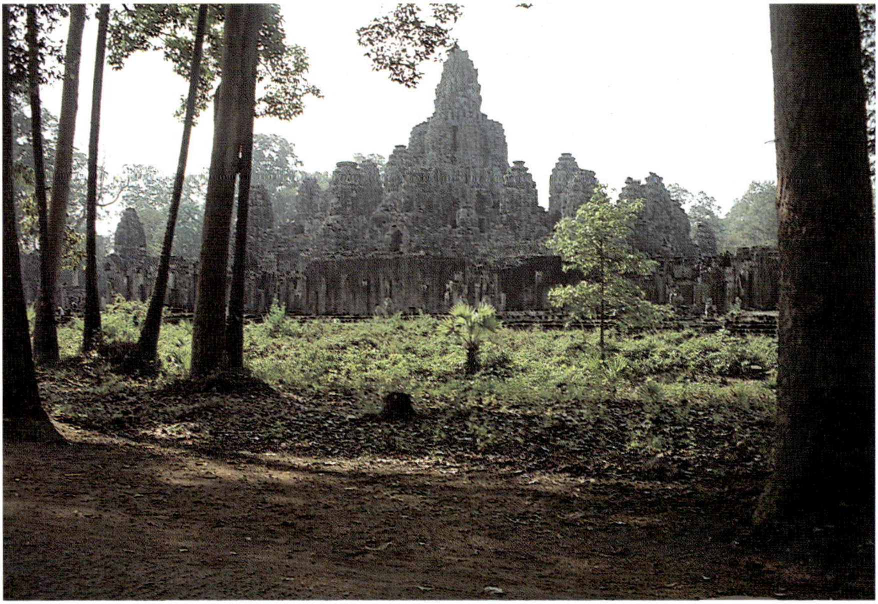

14. Bayon (Jayavarman VII, late twelfth century): general view

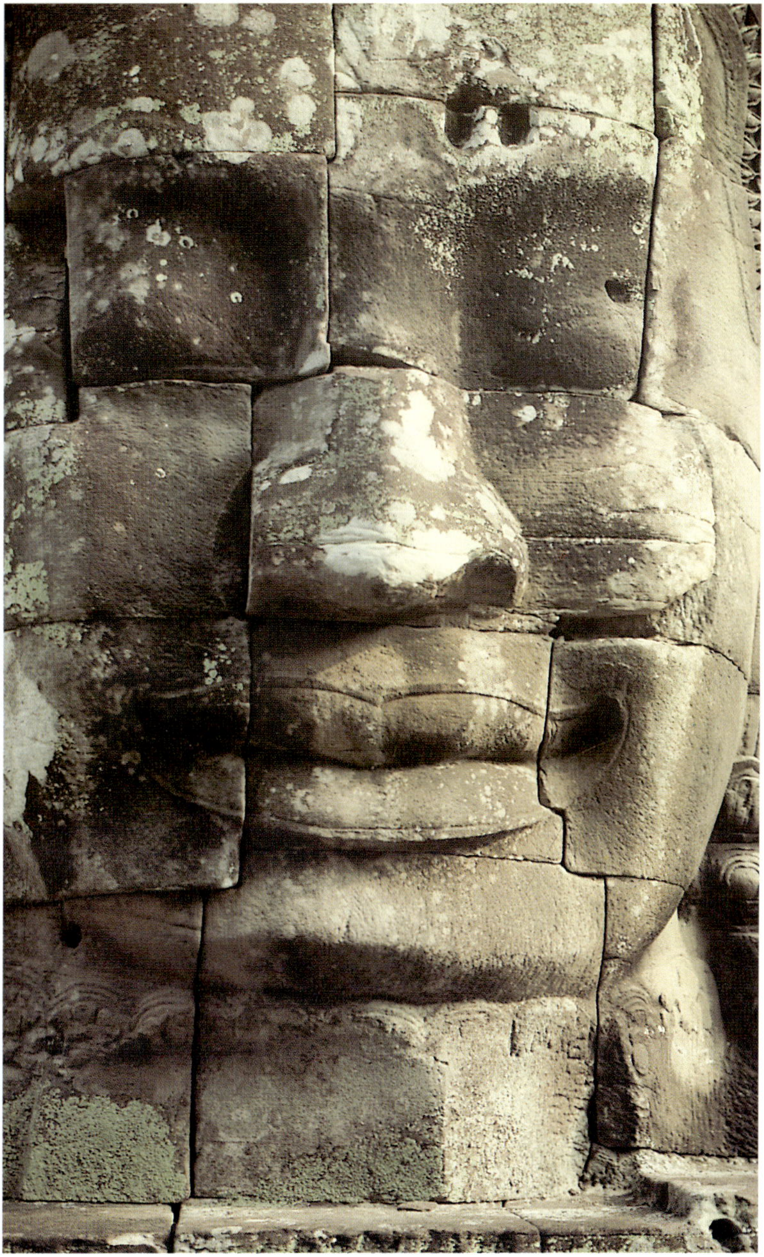

13. Angkor Thom: face of bodhisattva

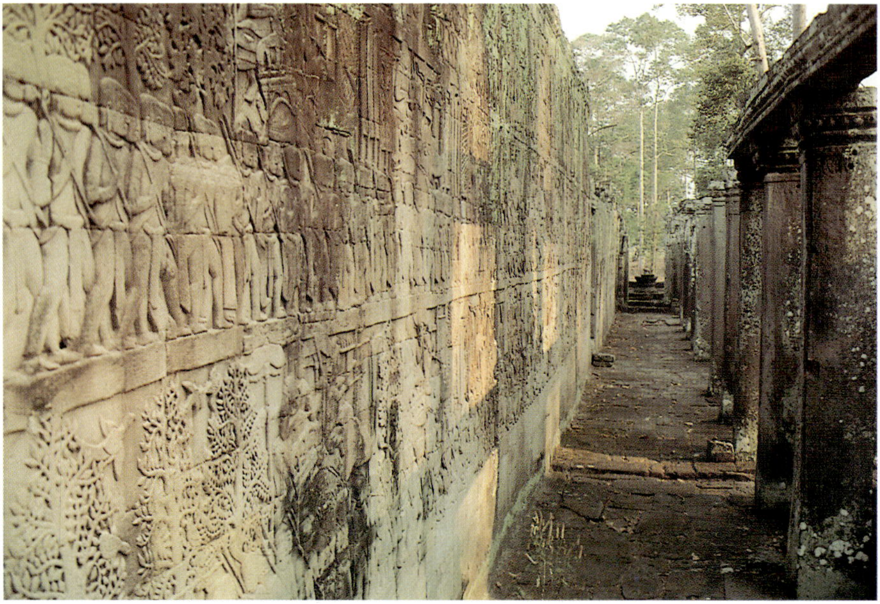

15. Bayon: inner corridor

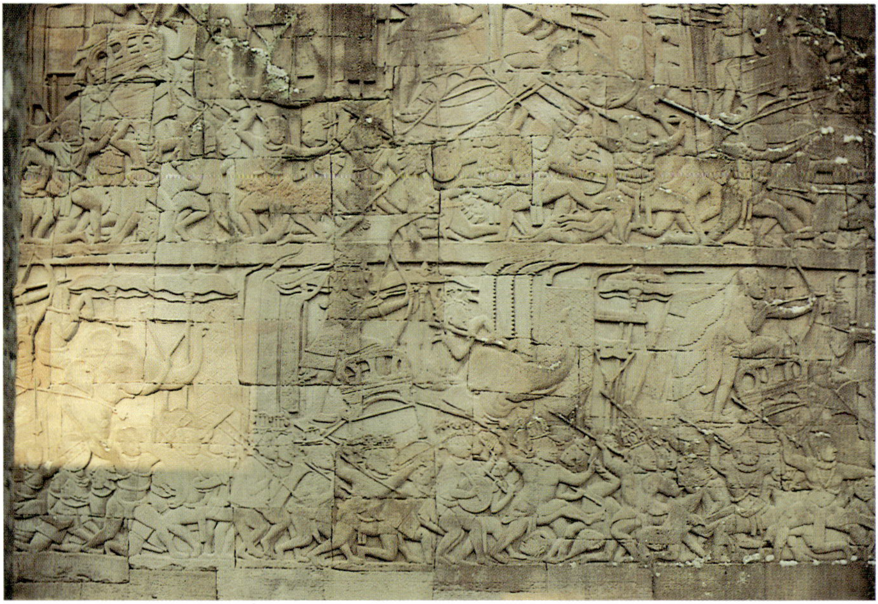

16. Bayon: detail of bas-relief

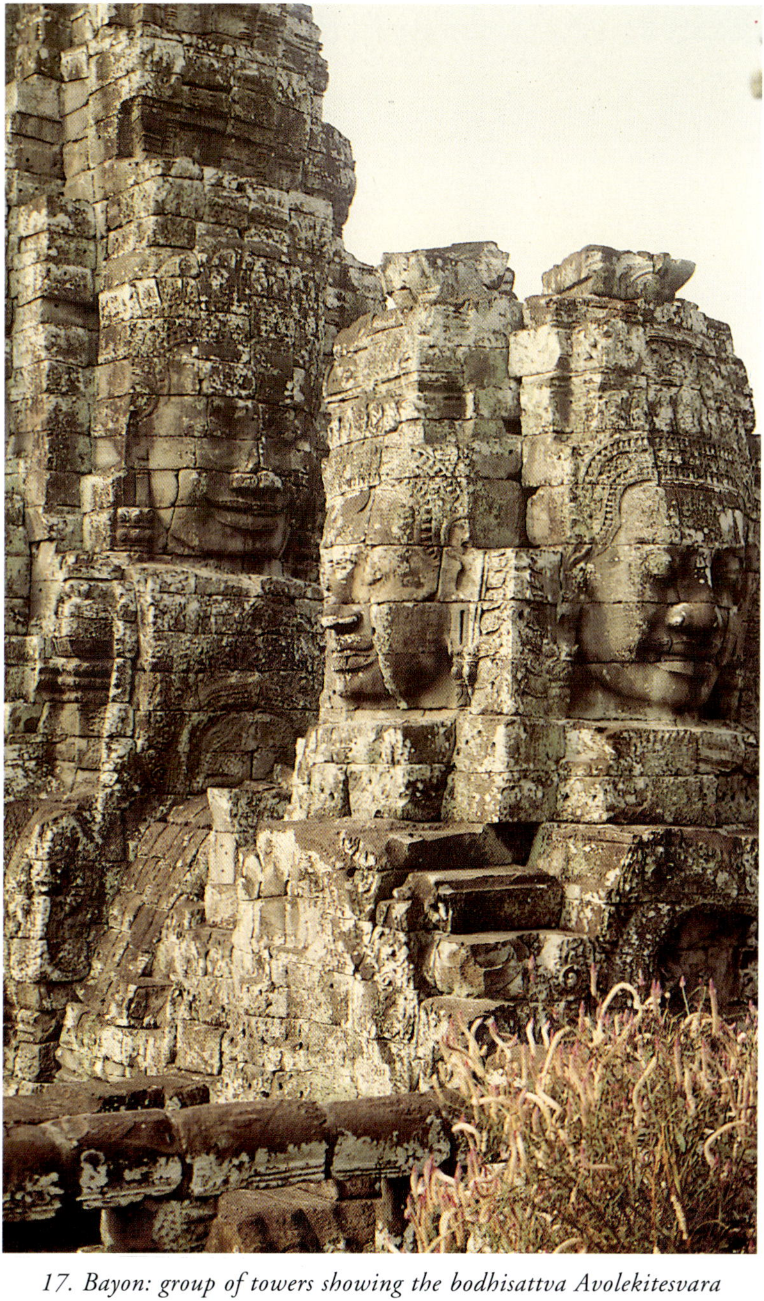

17. Bayon: group of towers showing the bodhisattva Avolekitesvara

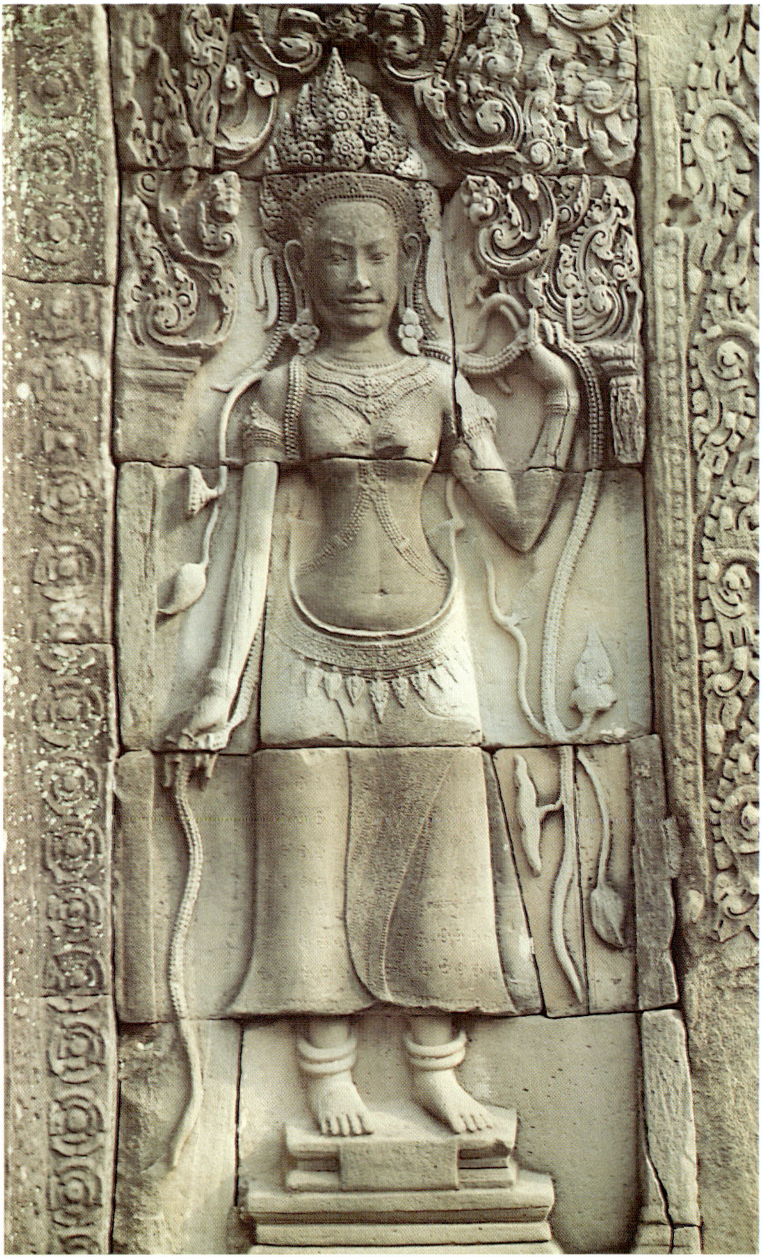

18. Bayon: full figure of an apsara

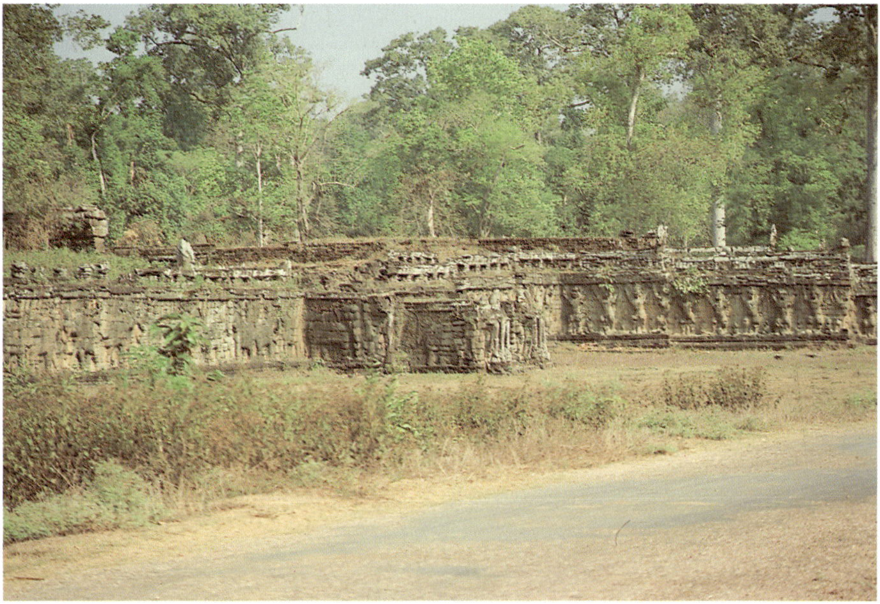
19. Angkor Thom: the royal palace terraces

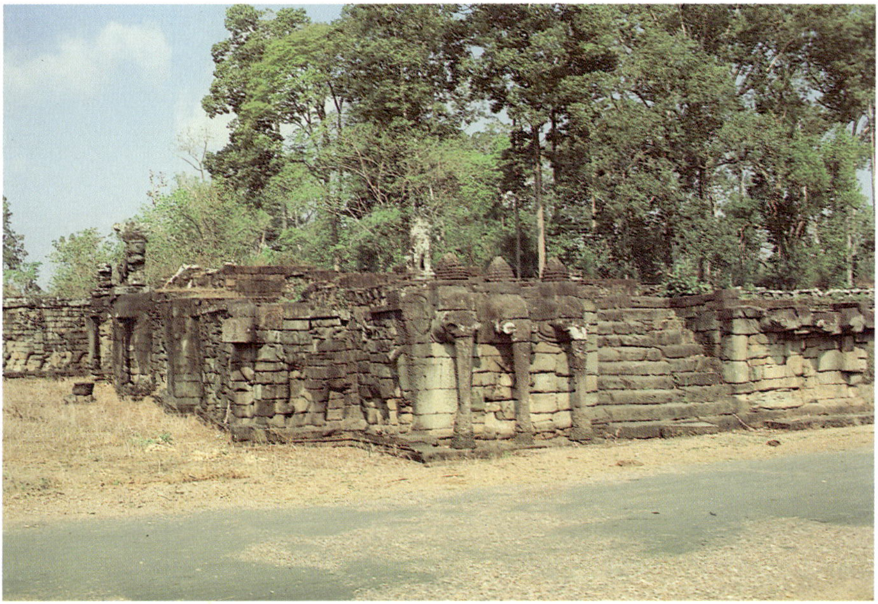
20. Angkor Thom: the elephant terrace at the royal palace

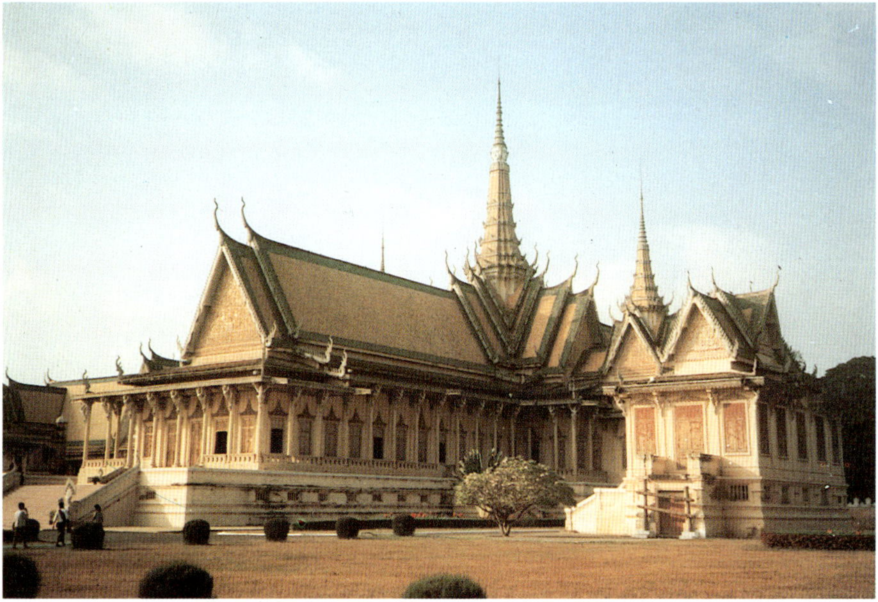

21. Phnom Penh: the royal palace

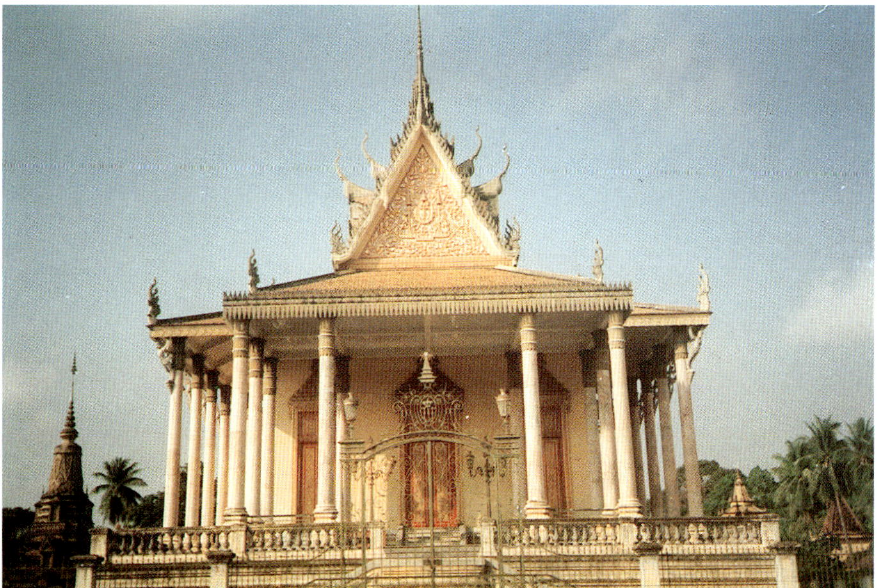

22. Phnom Penh: the so-called Silver Pagoda in the compound of the royal palace

CHAPTER I

I do not know if many men have had from childhood, as I have, a presentiment of their whole life. Nothing has happened to me that I have not dimly foreseen from my earliest years.

The ruins of Angkor! I remember so well a certain evening in April,[1] a little overcast, when as in a vision they appeared to me. It was in my "museum"—a tiny room allotted to my childish studies at the top of my parents' house—where I had gathered together a collection of shells, rare-plumaged birds, Oceanic arms and ornaments, everything that conjured up distant countries for me. For at this period it had been quite decided by my parents that I should remain at home and not roam about the world like my elder brother who had recently died out there in the Far East.[2]

That evening then, an ever inattentive schoolboy, I had shut myself in amongst these disturbing objects, for reverie rather than with the idea of completing my homework; and I was turning over some old and yellowed papers that had come back from Indo-China with the belongings of my dead brother. A few notebooks. Two or three Chinese books. And then an issue of I

1. Perhaps April 1865, when Loti was fifteen, since the beginning of the next chapter starts some thirty-five years later.

2. His brother Gustave died on 10 March 1865 in the Indian Ocean when returning from Saigon and news of his death reached Rochefort on 12 April.

know not what colonial review where the discovery of colossal ruins hidden in the depths of the forests of Siam was related.[3] There was one picture at which I stopped with a kind of thrill—showing great strange towers entwined with exotic branches, the temples of mysterious Angkor! Not for one moment did I doubt but that one day I should see them in reality, against all comers, in spite of impossibilities, in spite of prohibitions.

To think about it better I went and put my elbows on the ledge of the window in my museum. Of all the windows in the house one could see furthest from this one. In the foreground were the old roofs of the quiet neighbourhood; beyond, the centuries-old trees of the ramparts, and after that, at last, the river by which the ships made their way to the ocean.

And very distinctly at this time there came to me a presentiment of a life of travels and adventures, with magnificent, even somewhat fabulous moments, as for some oriental prince; and also some infinitely miserable times. In this future of mystery, greatly magnified by my childish imagination, I saw myself becoming a kind of legendary hero, an idol with feet of clay, fascinating thousands of people, worshipped by many, and by others suspect and reviled.

In order that my personality might be more romantic there needed some shadow in the renown I was imagining for myself. What could that shadow well be? Something fanciful and fearsome? Perhaps a pirate. Yes; it would not greatly have displeased me to be suspected of piracy on distant and scarcely known seas.

And then there appeared to me my own decline, and, much later, my return home with a weary heart, and with whitening hair. My family house, piously conserved, would have remained

3. Siamese sovereignty over the province of Siem Reap, in which lie the ruins of Angkor, had been acknowledged in the Franco-Siamese treaty of 1867. Siem Reap was returned to Cambodia in a further treaty in 1907. For a brief period in the Second World War the province, along with that of Battambang, was again Siamese.

unaltered; but here and there, pierced in the walls, hidden doors would lead to a palace of the thousand and one nights, filled with precious stones from Golconda, with all my fantastic loot.[4] And then, for the Bible was at that time my daily reading, I heard murmuring in my brain the verses of Ecclesiastes on the vanity of things.[5] Tired of the sights of the world and entering again, an old man, the same little museum of my childhood, I was repeating to myself: "I have tried all things; I have been everywhere, I have seen everything, etc." And amongst the many phrases already ringing sadly that came to lull me at my window was one that, I know not why, will remain for ever impressed upon my memory. It was this: "In the depths of the forests of Siam I have seen the evening star rise over the great ruins of Angkor."

A whistle, at the same time imperious and gentle, caused me suddenly to become again the little submissive child that in reality I had not ceased to be. It came from below, from the courtyard with its old walls garlanded with plants. I would have known it amongst a thousand; it was the usual summons of my father when I was discovered in some small transgression. And I replied, "I am up here, in my museum. Do you want me, father? Shall I come down?"

He must have come into my study and cast his eye over my unfinished homework.

"Yes, come down quickly, my boy, finish your Greek composition, if you want to be free after dinner to go to the circus."

4. This is an apt description of Loti's house in Rochefort, where the booty of his travels was grafted into houses adjacent to the family home kept as it was in his mother's time.

5. "Vanity of vanities, saith the Preacher, vanity of vanities; all is vanity... The thing that hath been, it is that which shall be; and that which is done is that which shall be done: and there is no new thing under the sun... All is vanity and vexation of spirit." Ecclesiastes I:2–14.

(I used to love the circus:[6] but I was toiling that year under the rod of a hated professor whom we called the Great Black Monkey[7] and my over-long homework was never finished.)

So, I got down to set myself to the composition. The courtyard, pleasant enough with its old low walls covered with roses and jasmine, struck me as too narrow, too enclosed, and the April twilight falling at this hour seemed unusually cloudy, even somewhat sinister; in my mind I had a vision of blue skies, wide spaces, the open sea—and the forests of Siam, out of which rose from amongst the banyans the towers of prodigious Angkor.

6. Loti always loved the circus, and even performed as an acrobat in the Etruscan Circus in Toulon in April 1876.

7. Loti and his schoolfriends, like schoolboys everywhere, gave mostly unflattering names to their teachers in the Collège de Rochefort. He details these in *Le Roman d'un Enfant* and *Prime Jeunesse*. A Monsieur Festy was apparently Great Black Monkey.

CHAPTER II

Saturday, 23rd November 1901.[1]

SOME thirty-five years later.

A warm, heavy, torrential rain is pouring from leaden clouds, deluging the trees and streets of a colonial town that smells of musk and opium. Half-naked Annamites[2] and Chinese hasten along, by the side of our soldiers whose faces are pale beneath their pith helmets. A noxious moist heat oppresses the lungs; the air seems to be the vapour of some cauldron in which perfumes are mingled with putrefaction.

And this is Saigon, a town I should never have seen, the very name of which once seemed to me mournful. For it was here that my brother (my elder by fifteen years) had come, like so many others of his generation, to absorb the germs of death.[3]

1. The battleship *Redoutable*, on which Julien Viaud (Loti) was serving as aide-de-camp to Vice-Admiral Pottier, left Nagasaki on 30 October 1901, arriving in Saigon on 19 November, and expecting to stay there about a month. In fact, it left on 8 December.

2. Vietnamese. Annam was the original name of the kingdom formed around Tonkin, the kingdom to the north, which became a French protectorate in 1883. Cochin-China broke away from Tonkin and by the seventeenth century was an independent kingdom occupying the central part of Vietnam, though under the French the name Cochin-China was given to their southern colony occupied in 1867. Annam, conquered by the French (1859-1883), became the name given to the central provinces.

3. Gustave Viaud spent three years in Papeete as a naval surgeon, and after

Today this Saigon of exile and languor is a familiar place enough. I have come now to think that I no longer hate it. When I came to it for the first time—already a little past the prime of life—how sadly strange and unfriendly I found its welcome.[4] But I have grown used to its leaden skies, to the exuberance of its unhealthy verdure, to the Chinese quaintness of its flowers, to its isolation in the midst of grassy plains strewn with tombs, to the little cat's eyes of its yellow women,[5] to all that constitutes its morbid and perverse attraction. Besides, I have already memories here, a semblance of a past; I have almost loved here; here, too, I have suffered much. And to its immense cemetery, overgrown with wild grasses, I have led many of my comrades-in-arms.

On my previous visits we were on perpetual alert, during warlike expeditions into Annam, Tonkin, and China; and it had not been possible to find time to make the deep plunge into the interior of the country, towards the ruins of Angkor. But at last, for once, I find myself at Saigon and at leisure. Our active naval service had terminated in the Gulf of Peking, and the heavy battleship to which I am attached is anchored here certainly for more than a month, alongside the nostalgic quay, near to that dismal and almost abandoned dockyard, where the earth is red as bloodstone beneath foliage that is too magnificently green.

And this evening, after so many years of waiting, I set out at length on my visit to the great ruins. The rain pours down on Saigon in the customary deluge. Everything is streaming with the tepid water. The carriage which takes me to the railway (my

---

home leave in Rochefort in 1862 was posted to Cochin-China. He fell ill with dysentery, embarked 3 March 1865 at Saigon on the *Alphée* to be repatriated, but died at sea seven days later.

4. Loti's first visit to Saigon was on 18 December 1883 (when he was thirty-three and hardly old), when he was recalled to France to explain his reports on the seizure of Hué; he was there again twice in 1885, and his most recent visit was in September 1900 on his way to Peking.

5. Loti was no liberal, and his lack of empathy with 'the yellow race' (a foolish if at the time generally used term, since it is largely untrue) comes out clearly in his reportage of his recent stay in China, published as *The Last Days of Peking*.

journey started banally) throws up cascades of reddish mud on naked torsos or the white linen clothes of passers-by. Around the station is a quarter that might be in the middle of China instead of a French colony.

The train starts; the carriages are stifling in spite of the soaking of the downpour. In the twilight, which quickens under the heavy clouds, we first have to traverse melancholy stretches of grassland which are studded with so many old rust-coloured Chinese mausoleums; the whole of the Plain of Tombs, where already everything is grey; and, were it not for the persistent heat, this November evening on this exotic steppe would be like one of our most misty evenings at home. And then the night overtakes us in the endless succession of the ricefields.

At the end of a two hours' journey the train stops. We are at My Tho,[6] which is the end of the line, the furthest point of this modest little colonial railway. Here the scene changes, as happens commonly in this region. All the clouds have melted in the sky, and the nocturnal blue stretches limpid, wonderful, with its scattering of stars. We are close by a great, tranquil river, the Mekong; hard by here a steamboat should be waiting to take me, first of all, to Cambodia, going upriver. The road which leads me there, along the river bank, is like the avenue of some trim park, only the trees that overhang it with their branches are larger than ours, and fireflies everywhere flicker their nimble, dancing lights. Peace and silence; the place would be perfect were it not for this eternal heaviness of the air and these enervating scents. A number of lights in a row amongst the greenery indicate the streets, or rather the paths, of the humble provincial town, which was laid out in one fell swoop on the level plain. And how can one describe the sadness, the pensive meditation, in the night-time, of these corners of France, of these pretences of the fatherland lost in the thick undergrowth of Asia, isolated from everything, even from the sea? Little groups of soldiers in white linen uniforms are taking their monotonous evening stroll along the

6. My Tho is some 60 km southwest of Saigon, on an arm of the Mekong delta.

road and, as they pass, I can detect some voices speaking with the accent of Gascony,[7] others with that of my native province.[8] Poor lads! Their mothers are waiting anxiously at far distant hearths; while they are going to spend here one or two of the best years of their lives. Perhaps they will leave behind them half-castes, who little by little infiltrate French blood into this unassimilable yellow people; then they will return home, made anaemic for a long time by this climate; or, perhaps, they will not return, but will go to sleep, with thousands of others, in the red earth of these cemeteries here, which are worrying in that they are so vast, and so overgrown with rank weeds.

The steamboat gets under way as soon as I am on board; we begin to go up the Mekong, keeping near to the banks, where the trees seem to stretch out like an intensely black curtain, and the fireflies continue their twinkling dances. Before we reach the border of the forests of Siam, I shall have to traverse the whole of Cambodia; but I shall stop at Phnom Penh,[9] the capital of the good King Norodom,[10] where I shall arrive by tomorrow night.[11]

7. Gascony was a former ducal province of France stretching from the Pyrenees to the Garonne, with its historical capital at Auch. It was united with Aquitaine in 1052 and shared its history thereafter.

8. Loti's Rochefort owes its existence to Colbert (at the time Louis XIV's superintendant of finance), who in 1666 ordered the creation of its port. It constituted part of the small historic province of Aunis which under Napoleonic changes became part of the Charente-Maritime (originally Charente-Inférieure) and Deux-Sèvres *départements*.

9. King Norodom decided in 1863 to move his capital to Phnom Penh; previously it has been at Udong.

10. Norodom I (1835-1904) had agreed to the French protectorate in 1863 and so was considered a good friend of France.

11. Loti in his Journal wrote a much briefer account for Saturday 23 November 1901: "Left Saigon with Osman [his valet] at 4.30 in the afternoon, under the excesses of a storm, in heavy and torrential rain. After two hours by train, arrived at My Tho. Left at dawn on a small steamboat waiting for us. The rain stopped. We began to go upstream on the great Cambodian river, between the mysterious banks of greenery, where the lights of fireflies wander." Similar reworkings and above all expansions were made to the original some ten years later when Loti was preparing the text for publication.

CHAPTER III

Sunday, 24th November 1901.

MY little steamboat has been making way all night against the current of the majestic river, travelling north. Daybreak finds us continuing the same peaceful navigation through this Indo-Chinese undergrowth, the endless curtains of which were so black under the stars, but have become so brilliant now in the sunlight. Banana trees, coconut palms, mangroves, bamboos, rushes, packed close together in a serried and endless mass. At first sight one might think the country was uninhabited; but looking more closely one sees how cunningly its opulent green cloak has been penetrated underneath by the human microbe. Here and there tracks, such as might be made by the beasts of the forest, emerge from beneath the trees and lead to the river. They are the first indication of the presence of villages. As we pass them at close quarters, the perfumes of the flowers become mingled with the stench of animals; a few poor huts can be seen buried among the branches, and human beings appear, very humble and, apparently, negligible, under the sovereign eternal verdure. Lean Annamites with bodies of the colour of saffron. Young women often gracious in body and countenance, but repulsive as soon as they smile and show their black lacquered teeth,[1] which make

1. Blackening the teeth was formerly common throughout mainland

the mouth look like a gloomy hole. A diminutive humanity, at once infantile and old, which has scarcely evolved since the time of the prehistoric ancestor, and has been hidden for centuries in the foliage of this tropical flora.

There are a number of native canoes on the river, each one fashioned out of a hollowed tree-trunk; and everywhere along the banks primitive kinds of fishing-tackle: varieties of traps made of reeds or bamboo, taking on different and distinctive shapes. For the most part they resemble huge cocoons, which, hardly emerging from the green confusion, plunge only half-way into the water. You might almost imagine that they were the chrysalises out of which these little yellow people were born: a sort of worm or mite, who here gnaw at the wonderful covering of the plains. And above so many outspread snares are the innumerable fisher-birds, long-legged, long-necked, with long, cruel beaks always ready for their prey. Men and wading birds alike waylay the myriads of silent, rudimentary lives which pass in the river; from all antiquity their flesh has been nourished on the colder flesh of fish.

More than once my pilot loses his way in the monotony of these banks, so endlessly alike, and strays into deceptive little tributaries, bordered always with the same curtains of verdure. And we run aground there and have to make our way back.

As evening approaches the human type changes. The few inhabitants of the banks, of whom we get glimpses through the reeds, are more Hindu, more Aryan in type; their eyes are large and *straight*, and the eyebrows well marked; moustaches shadow the lips of the men. The dwellings also are different, higher and raised on piles. We are no longer in Cochin-China. We have entered Cambodia.

And an hour after midnight we moor our boat to a quay before the town of Phnom Penh, which is asleep under the stars.

Southeast Asia; it was considered a sign of beauty, and distinguished humans from animals.

CHAPTER IV

Monday, 25th November 1901.

THE air here is already less oppressive than at Saigon, less charged with electricity and moisture. One feels more alive.

And a melancholy of a different kind emanates from this town, lost as it is in the interior of a land-bound country, without ships, without sailors, without animation of any sort. It is comparatively only a few years since King Norodom confided his country to France,[1] and already everything that we have built at Phnom Penh has taken on an age-worn air under the scorching sun. The fine straight roads we traced here, along which no one passes, are green with weeds. It might be one of those colonies of antiquity, the charm of which lies in abandonment and silence.

Today, though, is the third day of the traditional water festival,[2] and in the evening, as the sun turns to a coppery red, the banks of the river suddenly become animated. In one of the royal junks, the prow of which represents the enormous head of some monster from a Cambodian dream, I watch, in company with a score or so French men and women living in exile here at

1. Thirty-eight years previously.

2. The annual water festival, usually in the second half of November, marked the end of the rainy season and the beginning of the cool, when the waters began to go down.

Phnom Penh, the parade of the long racing galleys. They go past in a furious eddy of spray, manipulated by half-naked men, who paddle standing, with striking postures, shouting encouraging cries.[3]

3. Another example of how this was expanded can be seen in Loti's Journal entry for 25 November: "Day in Phnom Penh. The third day of the water festival. In the evening, on the banks of the great river, in a boat belonging to the king, the prow of which is a huge monster's head, I watch the joists of galleys passing by. Long, thin galleys, propelled by some twenty standing men, bare-chested, shouting and rowing together. Long galleys passing by in a furious eddy of foam. The air is already less oppressive than in Saigon, less charged with electricity and rain. It feels better here."

CHAPTER V

Tuesday, 26th November 1901.

STANDING back from the bank of the river stretch the vast quarters of the king, wrapped in silence. With their denuded courts they form a kind of clearing in the middle of this country, by the side of this town so overgrown with trees, and the roads of reddish earth which surround them are pitted with broad footprints from the daily outing of the elephants.

Today at half past six o'clock, wandering alone in the early morning sunshine, I enter the gate of one of the courtyards of the palace; a very large courtyard, paved white. In the middle, isolated in the bright emptiness, is a slim temple of white and gold, the roof of which bristles with golden spikes, and isolated also at either side of this little solitude are two high golden bell-turrets, extraordinarily pointed, which support rockeries decked with orchids and a thousand rare plants. I can see no one, anywhere. But the silence here is of a peculiar kind; a humming sound mingles with it in an undertone without disturbing it, a vague, aerial music which at first escapes definition; it is the concert of little silvery bells suspended at each point of the bell-turrets and of the roofs; the least breath of air that passes makes them tinkle softly.

The temple is quite new,[1] the whiteness of its marble and its glistening gold dazzle one. Its windows are decorated with copings of gold, which, against the snowy background of the walls, stand out like pieces of fine jewellery that terminate in tapering spires. Its roofs, covered with gilded ceramics, are ornamented at every corner with finials of extraordinary length, which curve and become upright, menacing in all directions. Compared with these, the finials of the Chinese temples appear truly rudimentary, hardly begun; it is as if many giant bulls have had their horns removed to decorate this strange temple. The different peoples of the yellow race have been haunted for centuries by this conception of decorative roof finials for their religious edifices, but it has been left to the Cambodians to surpass them all in extravagance.

Steps are approaching, heavy steps, and three elephants appear.[2] Paying no heed to me they cross the courtyard with a knowing, sedulous air, as of people aware of what they have to do. The sound of their march and of the bells hung at their collars breaks for a moment into the aeolian concert which falls discreetly from above, and then, as soon as they have gone, the musical silence returns, exquisite here in the purity and comparative freshness of the morning.

The open doors of the temple invite me to enter.

On its ceiling, on its walls, over-bright golds glisten everywhere, and my footsteps resound on plaques of bright new silver with which the temple is paved throughout. There are still countries then, where, in our times, men think to build such sanctuaries!

1. The Silver Pagoda, as it is generally if inaccurately known, in the second enclosure of the Royal Palace, was, like the palace itself, recent; it was originally built in 1892 by King Norodom.

2. Loti's Journal states: "Two elephants came out. And a small procession of monks in their lemon-yellow robes with orange belts, under huge parasols." His written-up version improves on the original by adding an elephant and increasing his solitude by eliminating the monks.

Almost immediately, through a different door, four small creatures appear before me, all of them young, all of them slender, with hair cut short like boys, and a gardenia flower placed over their ears. The beautiful silks which cover them, outlining their scarcely-formed breasts, indicate them to be palace maidens, ballet-dancers beyond a doubt, for that is apparently all there is at the court of old King Norodom. To the movement which I make to withdraw, they reply by a charming, timid sign, as if to say: "No, stay where you are; you are not disturbing us." And I thank them with a bow. This human courtesy which we have learnt at opposite ends of the earth, and of which just now we have vaguely made the exchange, is moreover the only notion we have in common. In the course of my life I had met with many women little better than dolls or toys, but never before had I come across the Cambodians *at home*; and I watch these four as, with silent steps and easy, unaffected grace, they move about over the silver floor. From early childhood their bodies, all their limbs, have been made supple by those long, ritual dances, which are the custom here on feast days and at funerals. Who brings them so early to this temple? What childish sorrow? And what kinds of prayers are formulated by their little souls, that are revealed now, anxious, in their eyes?

The heat is already oppressive as I return to the French quarter, to look for shade on board my little steamboat moored against the bank. Prostration and silence in the streets, laid out so straight but so empty, where the weeds encroach upon the pavements. Save for some naked Cambodian convicts, who, careless and happy, are watering the lawns of the strangely-flowered gardens, I meet nobody. The capital of King Norodom has gone to sleep till the close of the day, under the dazzling brilliance of its sun. And clearly this little corner of France, which has been grafted here, does not seem viable, such an air of decrepitude and abandonment has it taken on after only a few years.

At three o'clock in the afternoon I make ready to continue my journey towards the ruins of Angkor, going up the Mekong.[3] Phnom Penh disappears at once; and the prodigious Asiatic undergrowth envelops us again between its two profound curtains. At the same time there is revealed, all around, an animal life of impetuous intensity. On the banks, which we almost brush in passing, whole armies of fisher-birds are standing on the look-out: pelicans, egrets, and marabouts. Sometimes the air is blackened with flights of crows. In the distance arise little clouds of green dust, which as they approach are seen to be flights of innumerable parakeets. Here and there the trees are full of monkeys, and you can see their long tails hanging in lines like a fringe from all the branches.

From time to time, human habitations in an isolated group. Always a long shaft of gold dominates them, pointing into the sky: the temple.

My men have asked that they might be allowed to provision themselves with fruits for the journey, so I call a halt, at the hour of twilight, at a large village built on piles all along the bank of the river. Some smiling Cambodians come forward at once offering fresh coconuts and bunches of bananas. And while the bargaining proceeds, an enormous red moon rises beyond, over the infinitude of the forests.

Night falls as we resume our journey. Cries of owls, cries of beasts of prey, an infinite concert of all kinds of musical insects, delirious with the nocturnal frenzy in the inextricable verdure.

And then, later on, the waters spread out so much that we no longer see the banks. We are entering the immense lake formed here every year after the rainy season by the powerful river, which periodically inundates the low-lying plains of Cambodia and a part of the forests of Siam. Not a breath of wind. As if we were floating on oil, we trace, in gliding over this feverous lake,

3. Properly speaking, Loti does not go up the Mekong from Phnom Penh to reach Siem Reap and Angkor, but up one of its tributaries, the Tonle Sap River, leading to the great lake, the Tonle Sap.

smooth folds which the moon silvers. And the warm air, which we cleave rapidly, is encumbered with clouds of scatterbrained insects, which assemble in a whirlwind at the sight of our lanterns, and rain down on us: gnats, mosquitoes, mayflies, beetles, dragonflies.

Towards midnight, when we had just got off to sleep and lay, half-naked, with the windows open, we were visited without warning by a swarm of enormous black beetles, covered with prickles like a chestnut, but otherwise inoffensive, which crawled very rapidly over us, exploring our chest and arms.

CHAPTER VI

Wednesday, 27th November 1901.

ON the lake, large as a sea, here comes the sunrise. And in a few minutes everything takes on colour. On the eastern horizon the limpid air turns bright pink, and a line of beautiful Chinese green indicates the endless continuation of the inundated forest. In contrast, on the western horizon—where the shore is too far off to be seen—there is a massing of sombre, chaotic, terrifying objects, which weigh upon the waters—things which hold together and remain upright, like mountainous masses, and stand out as sharply as real peaks against the clear sky; but which seem, nevertheless, to be on the point of collapsing as formidably as those of the end of the world. The whole of this heaped-up mass is ravined, caverned, contorted, with deep shadows in its folds, and lights of reddish copper on its outcrops. And right above it, as if it had been placed there, the old, dead moon, a large full moon the colour of tin, begins to fade before the sun which rises opposite. All this western horizon would be a frightening sight to avoid looking at, if one did not know what in fact it is: a storm appearing a hundred times more terrible than ours, which broods there as if sleeping, and in all probability will not break.

It was to this we owed the heat and the kind of enervating electric tension which had oppressed us towards the end of the night. From experience of these climates we had guessed before seeing it that somewhere or other in the air there was a bogey of this kind. But now, it begins to lose shape, is attenuated, so that it no longer gives the appearance of consistency, and we breathe more and more freely in proportion as it all gradually dissolves. At present there are a few negligible clouds; soon after there remains nothing but a light vapour which does no more than cover with a warm mist the western side of this little sea over which we travel alone.

Not a junk in sight, no more sign of man than before his first appearance amongst the terrestrial fauna. But here and there long trails of a pinkish-white streak the greenish waters saturated with organic substances. They are flocks of pelicans, sleeping as they float.

Until the middle of the day, we continue our progress over this motionless lake, which gleams like polished tin. On the eastern horizon what looks to be a kind of green foam stretches endlessly, always the same; tall trees, the trunks of which are entirely submerged, so that the tops alone rise out of the water. It is only an illusory shore, for beneath the verdure the lake continues to spread over indefinite distances. It is no more than the boundary of the deeper waters in which the vegetation would lose its footing.

Thirty leagues,[1] forty leagues of submerged forest pass by in this way while we continue our peaceful course towards the north. An immense zone, useless during this season for men, but a prodigious reservoir of animal life: shades full of snares and ambushes, of ferocious beaks and claws, of little venomous teeth, of tiny sharpened barbs for deadly bites. There are branches that bend beneath the weight of grave marabouts in repose; and trees so laden with pelicans that in the distance they seem to be covered with large pale-pink flowers.

When, in the course of our navigation, we almost touch this forest of eternal green, the guests in the branches become

1. A league is a variable measure of distance, of approximately four kilometres.

alarmed and take flight. And then, at close quarters, we see skeins of climbing plants reeled off from the trees, linking them to one another, so that the whole is bound together to form a single inextricable mass.

At about one o'clock, we cast anchor in the shade of a little bay, enclosed with uncontrollable greenery. This, it appears, is the place where the large sampans, ordered in advance from the chief of the nearest village, on the way to Angkor, will come to find me. The little steamboat which has carried me to this point would not in any case be able to proceed further through the forest.[2]

They appear at about six o'clock in the evening, these roofed sampans, emerging one after the other from under the masses of creepers. The large red sun has just set when I take my place in one, with my French servant, my Cambodian interpreter, my Chinese boy, and our light wanderers' baggage. And then we begin to thrust our way with the oars into the labyrinth of trees, into the heart of the submerged forest which closes over us. At the same time the night comes to envelop us, almost suddenly, without any twilight.

The region which we are now about to traverse is transformed into a lake only for six months of the year. Soon the waters will subside, and the earth will reappear and proceed hastily to cover itself with pasture. And men will return to build their huts for the dry season, leading back their flocks and followed by the inevitable train of tigers and monkeys. A pastoral life will resume its place here until the next rains.

2. Loti eliminates the meeting here of his superior, Vice-Admiral Pottier, presumably in order to make the journey sound more remote and isolated. His Journal states: "At one o'clock, the *Lutin,* the King of Cambodia's yacht, which brought the admiral here, appears, and is waiting for him... We also anchored here, to wait for the sampans which took the admiral to Angkor, to return, and come from the forest. They appear about six in the evening... The admiral, only just on board the *Lutin* which is going to take him back to Cambodia and Saigon, read a sealed despatch which I had brought him. It was our official orders to return to France, with the *Redoutable*, next March..."

All these large trees, immersed up to the forking of their branches, are not distinguishable in the darkness from our oaks and beeches; and it might be an inundated country of a climate such as our own, were it not for this oppressive heat, this excess of scents everywhere, this excess of rustling sounds, this plethora of sap and life. The sky is covered anew with storm-clouds, and the atmosphere again becomes overwhelming. The night is starless and moonless. In this area, there are no silhouettes of palms. The great black tufts which follow one another in an indefinite procession during our journey are like the tops of our trees at home, although they are of unknown varieties. Despite the night you can see them repeated in the darkened mirror of the waters, and their vague reversed reflections somehow seem to reinforce for us the feeling of inundation, of abnormality, of cataclysm. All the time, as we go along, we hit against the thick foliage, and lizards that were lying asleep, mayflies in myriads, little snakes or else grasshoppers fall on our shoulders. Often our rowers lose their way, call to one another with lugubrious Asiatic cries, and change their course. The ruins which we are going to visit are truly admirably guarded by such a forest.

At the end of some two hours, however, we succeed in emerging from beneath the trees, and enter a marsh, amongst gigantic grasses. Here slumbers a very narrow river which we begin to go up, brushing against reeds and plants of every sort. The night grows ever darker. As we pass we disturb great birds which take flight, or perhaps an otter, or some doe which we can hear making its escape with light bounds. And at last, at about ten o'clock, while our boatmen continue their unceasing rowing, we stretch ourselves out under our mosquito nets and at once fall into a trusting sleep.

CHAPTER VII

Thursday, 28th November 1901.

IT is about two o'clock in the morning. We are half-awakened, but deliciously, by a sound of slow, soft, completely unfamiliar, and such strange music, neither too far off nor too near—flutes, dulcimers, zithers, and, it would seem, too, peals of little bells and silvery gongs giving rhythm to the melody in an undertone. At the same time we become conscious that the music of the oars has ceased and the sampan no longer moves. Here, then, is the end of our journey by water, and we are moored, no doubt, against the bank ready to disembark at sunrise. The music continues, monotonously, repeating over and over again the same phrases, which are not fatiguing but soothing. And we soon fall asleep again, after murmuring to ourselves, in these moments of being half-awake: "Good! We have reached some village in Siam and there is a night festival in the temple in honour of the local gods."

Half-past six in the morning. We awake again, but for good this time, for it is day. Between the planks which shelter us we see filtering rays of pink light. The music has not ceased. It is there still, always soft and always the same, but mingled now with the morning clarion of cocks, and the sounds of daily life about to start again.

It is enchanting to look outside. If the vegetation of the submerged forest, on which our eyes closed, recalled that of our climate, here a tropical flora of the utmost extravagance is displayed in all varieties of palms, of huge green fronds, of great green fans. We are in front of a village, on a little river with flowery banks. Through the reeds the rising sun shoots its golden arrows everywhere. Little thatched houses built upon piles form a line along a pathway of fine sand. Men and women, half-naked, slender, with copper-coloured bodies, move around amongst the verdure. They go backwards and forwards a little out of curiosity to see us; but they look on discreetly smiling and kindly. The flowers perfume the air: an odour of jasmine, of gardenia, of tuberose. In the clear light of dawn this simple morning coming and going seems like a scene of the early ages, when man still had tranquillity. And, too, used as we had become to the ugliness of the daughters of Annam, who see only through slit eyelids, through two little oblique holes, what a change it seems, and what a comfort, to come amongst a people who open their eyes more or less as we open our own.

And we put foot to earth in Siam.* Beyond, under a shed with a roof of mats which constitutes the temple, the musicians of the night, who for the moment are silent, are squatting by the side of their dulcimers, flutes, and zithers. They had given all this concert of theirs for some humble Buddhist pictures daubed in blue, red and gold, which are hung there, before which are also fading offerings of flowers: lotus, waterlilies and jasmine.

And now arrive my ox-carts, ordered since yesterday from the chief of the district; five carts, for there is not room in one for more than a single person, who sits back to back with the drover. They resemble a sort of mandolin, mounted on wheels and drawn by the long neck, which is curved like the prow of a gondola.

*** The writer knows, of course, that under an arrangement recently made with Siam the territory of Angkor has been ceded to Cambodia—in other words, to France.**[1]

1. This is Loti's own note, which appeared when the text was first published in 1912. See note 3 on page 6.

We have to hurry our departure in order to arrive at Angkor before the midday heat. At the outset of our journey we follow the course of the narrow river along a sandy path, bordered with reeds and flowers. Above us is a colonnade of tall coconut palms, from which hang garlands of creepers, decked with clusters of flowers. There is an exquisite morning freshness under these huge palms. We pass through villages, peaceful and pleasing as in the golden age, where the inhabitants watch us go by with smiles of shy goodwill. The people seem ever more mixed with Indian blood, for many of the young women have large, black eyes, darkened like those of nautch-girls.

After an hour we stop at Siem Reap, almost a town, but quite Siamese in character, with its little houses always perched on piles, and its temple bristling with golden finials. It has a post office, rather a rustic one, where one may frank letters with stamps bearing the likeness of King Chulalongkorn;[2] and a little telegraph office also, for a telegram is brought to me, couched in these words:

> *"Resident Superior of Phnom Penh to Governor of Siem Reap. Will you please inform M. Pierre Loti that he will find four elephants at Kampong Luong on his return."*

It is what I was hoping for. I had formulated a request to the good King Norodom asking if he could place four elephants at my disposal in order that, when I had made the pilgrimage to Angkor, I might visit the temple where rest the ashes of the queen mother of Cambodia, in the midst of the forest.

On leaving Siem Reap our ox-carts turn away from the river and follow another sandy road which plunges right into the forest. And then suddenly there is an end to the tall green fronds above our heads; for all this vegetation of coconut and areca

2. King Chulalongkorn, Rama V (1835–1910) reigned from 1868 to his death. It was during his reign the the Post and Telegraph Department was set up and postage stamps were first introduced.

palms is confined to the banks of the river. We make our way now under foliage similar to that of our own climates, only the trees that bear it would be a little giant-like compared with ours. In spite of so much shade, the heat, as the sun climbs in the sky, becomes every minute more oppressive. Following the ill-defined road through the vast forest and impenetrable jungle, our carts jog along in time with the trotting of the oxen between two banks of thickets or ferns. And the prudent monkeys climb to the highest of the branches.

When, at the end of some two hours' travelling through the forest in this fashion, we were beginning, what with the jolting and the rocking and the heat, to succumb to sleep, the fabulous town suddenly appeared before our eyes.

In front of us an open space appears; a marsh overgrown with grasses and water lilies, then a broad gangway which liberates us at last from the forest, through which we had been travelling in confinement; and, further on, beyond the stagnant waters, a number of towers, in the form of a tiara, towers of grey stone, immense dead towers, outlined against the pale luminosity of the sky. Yes! I recognize them at once. They are indeed the towers in the old picture which had so troubled me once upon a time, on an April evening, in my childhood museum. I am in the presence of mysterious Angkor!

Yet somehow I do not feel the emotion that I should have expected. It is probably too late in life, and I have seen too many of these remains of the great past, too many temples, too many palaces, too many ruins. Besides it is all so blurred, as it were, under the glare of the daylight; it is difficult to see it because it is too bright. And, above all, midday is drawing near with its lassitude, its invincible somnolence.

The colossal ramparts and the towers that have just appeared to us, like some mirage of the torrid heat, are not the town itself, but only Angkor Wat, its principal temple near which we are supposed to camp this evening. The town, Angkor Thom, so we are advised, lies further away, immense and indeterminate, buried under the tropical forest.

Leading to this phantom basilica is a bridge of remote ages, built of Cyclopean blocks, which crosses a pool, choked with reeds and water lilies. Two monsters, corroded by time and bearded with lichen, guard the entrance to it. It is paved with broad flagstones, which sink and slope, and in places seem almost on the point of slipping into the greenish waters. Drawn by our oxen we cross it, almost asleep. On the further side opens a gateway, surmounted by turrets like tiaras, and flanked by two gigantic cobra serpents which rear up and display, in the form of a fan, their seven stone heads.[3]

And, having passed through this gateway, we are within the outer enclosure, which has a circumference of more than a league: a mournful, enclosed solitude, resembling a neglected garden, with brambles entwined with fragrant jasmine, out of which rise, here and there, ruins of little towers, statues with closed eyes, or the multiple heads of the sacred cobra. The sun is scorching now that we have left the shade of the thick branches. An avenue paved with grey stones stretches before us its diminishing line, leading straight to the sanctuary, the gigantic mass of which now dominates everything. A sinister avenue passing through an over-mysterious little desert and leading to ruins under a deathly sun. But as we draw nearer to this temple, which we had thought vowed to a perpetual silence, a sound of soft music seems to come more distinctly to our ears, which are a little bothered, if the truth be told, by the feverish heat and the need for sleep. For all that, it is clearly a sound of music, distinct from the concert of the insects and the creaking of our ox-carts. It resembles vaguely the sound of innumerable human voices chanting a slow psalmody. Who can sing in this way among the ruins in spite of the overpowering heaviness of midday?

At the very foot of this crushing mass of sculptured stone, of terraces and stairways, and towers that soar into the sky, we come upon the village from where these chanted prayers arise.

3. These are the naga, the mythical semi-divine serpents which inhabit the waters and rule over the land.

Overhung by a few tall, frail palm trees are little houses on piles, constructed very lightly of wood and mats, with elegant little festooned windows which are quickly adorned with curious heads to see us arrive. These people have shaven crowns and are all clothed in the same lemon-coloured robe, beneath an orange-coloured drapery. They chant in a subdued voice, and continue to watch us without interrupting their tranquil litany.

It is a very singular village this, without women, without cattle, without crops, nothing but these singers, yellow in face, and clothed in two shades of yellow. About two hundred monks from Cambodia and Siam, dedicated to the guardianship of the sacred ruins, live there in continual prayer, chanting night and day before this heap of titanic blocks piled up into a mountain.

The arrival of our carts, however, and our oxen and drovers interrupts for a moment their monotonous dreaming. To welcome us two or three of them come down from their high perched houses, and, with their heads shining in the sunlight, advance to meet us, without haste or embarrassment, in the heat which now falls perpendicularly upon the earth, and which the earth sends back more unhealthy and more humid.

They offer us as lodging the large shelter provided for the use of the faithful during pilgrimages. Raised on piles like their houses, it consists of lattice floor with a thatch roof upheld by pillars of reddish wood. It has no wall, and to screen us, night and day, we have only the transparent curtains of our mosquito nets. By way of furniture there is nothing but an old Buddhist altar, with gods of fading gold, before which little heaps of ash bear witness to the burning of many an incense stick.*

We lie down there on mats, behind our hastily hung muslin curtains, happy to be able at last to stretch ourselves some five or six feet above the ground where the snakes crawl, happy to feel that our heads are protected by a real roof, under which there is,

* Since Angkor came into the possession of France a house has apparently been built after the fashion of an Indian bungalow for the accommodation of European visitors.

if not coolness, at least a deep shade. And seeking the shade also, the oxen lie down beneath our house, on the moist, warm earth.

If there had been any air it would have come to us from all parts, even from below, for the floor has gaps. But there is none anywhere at this hour when everything is burning, motionless and languid. The midday torpor extinguishes all sounds and congeals things.The eternal psalmody of the monks, even the murmur of the insects seem to be muffled and to slow down. Through the muslin, as through a fog, we still see, quite close, quite close indeed, the enormous foundations of the temple, the towers of which we can imagine vanishing above in the white incandescence. The heaviness and the mystery of these immense ruins which fill half the sky disturb me still more as my eyes close, and it is only when sleep is on the point of making me lapse into unconsciousness that I recognize as finally accomplished my desire of long ago, that I feel I have indeed arrived at Angkor.

I must have been asleep two or three hours when by degrees I began to wake. What can I have been dreaming of? I seemed to be in a nameless country, where everything was sad and dark. Near me, on a white beach before a confused and black sea, were moving the silhouettes of human beings, whom, perhaps, I may have loved in some previous existence—who knows?—for my heart sank somewhat when the broad light of reality, returning suddenly, drove them into a non-existence beyond recall. Where am I? In what region of the earth am I opening my eyes again? The air is hot with a moist, close heat, as if I had been sleeping above a basin of boiling water. There is shade above my head, but around me, framed by this kind of fringe which falls from the thatched roof, are things close to which shimmer in an excess of vivid light: they are leaves bathed in sunshine, and interminable rows of grey stones, the reflection of which dazzles me. And in the air there is a sound of chanting, a kind of lamentation in an unknown rhythm. Ah, the litany of the monks. And these grey stones? Yes, I remember: the colossal stone foundations of the ruins. I have been sleeping since midday at the foot of the great temple of Angkor, in this clearing, guarded by moats and low walls, and surrounded on all sides in the silence of the thick, green shroud of the surrounding tropical forest.

It is half-past three, the hour when everything awakes here, after the daily torpor. Beneath the open-work floor I can hear the oxen moving, and the drovers beginning again to talk. The flies buzz in a crescendo, and the chanting of the monks grows louder.

There is no cloud in the sky, no threatening storm. The whole vault is resplendent, palely blue, above the enormous towers. There seems no doubt but that the tropical soaking is going to spare us again for the evening. Let us, then, put the oxen again to the carts; instead of visiting the temple, I shall rather go and see the town, which lies over there under the shroud of trees. It is some distance away, this buried city. Whereas there are scarcely ten metres between my suspended dwelling and the steps leading to the first galleries of the sanctuary; it will be an easy thing to visit it at any time, however much it rains.

With the same creaking of wheels, the same rocking slowness, we cross once more the enclosed copse, passing through the entrance portico and over the bridge where, like sentinels, the great serpents watch with their seven heads.

And, following the vague jungle pathways we plunge again beneath the infinite covering of the forest. The heat, which weighs as heavily as ever upon our shoulders, becomes all at once shady and moist. Clouds of mosquitoes envelop us, and we breathe that peculiar kind of malaria which induces the "fever of the woods."

We had been travelling for about an hour through the uninterrupted forest, amongst unfamiliar flowers, when the ramparts of the town at last rose before us, themselves wrapped in the deep green night of the forest, beneath the entanglement of branches. They were formerly defended by a moat measuring a hundred metres across, which earth and dead leaves filled up, and they had a circumference of more than four leagues. As we come upon the ramparts now they look like rocks, so high and worn are they, so deformed by the patient labour of roots, so overgrown with brambles and ferns. The Gate of Victory,[4] under which we are about to pass, might at first sight be mistaken for the entrance to a cavern overhung with creepers.

In epochs that are uncertain, this town, buried now for many centuries, was one of the glories of the world. Just as the old Nile, by virtue merely of its silt, had caused the creation in its valley of a marvellous civilization, so here the Mekong, spreading each year its waters, had deposited a richness, and prepared the way for the luxurious empire of the Khmers. It was probably in the time of Alexander the Macedonian,[5] that a people, emigrating from India, came and settled on the banks of this great river, after subjugating the timid natives—men with little eyes, worshippers of the serpent. The conquerors brought with them the gods of Brahmanism and the beautiful legends of the Ramayana; and as their opulence increased on this fertile soil, they built gigantic temples, carved with a thousand figures.

Later—some centuries later, one cannot say how many, for the existence of this people is much effaced from the memory of

4. Angkor Thom had five monumental gateways: one each in the centre of the perimeter wall, at the cardinal points, leading to Jayavarman VII's focal point at the centre, the Bayon, and a fifth gate, on the eastern side, known as the Gate of Victory, which led to the royal palace, the Phimeanakas, and what are now called the terraces of the leper king and the elephants. Loti did not in fact pass through the Gate of Victory when moving from Angkor Wat to Angkor Thom, but through the nameless southern gate by the tenth century Baksei Chamkrong, the first temple-mountain to be built of durable materials and dedicated to Shiva.

5. Alexander the Great (356–323 B.C.), King of Macedon, conqueror of Egypt, Persia, and the Punjab. The arrival of the Khmers in the region is the subject of much debate; they were probably settled at the beginning of the Christian era. The Indianization of the Khmers was a long and slow process of uncertain dating. An early state known from Chinese chronicles as Funan existed from the third to the sixth centuries. The earliest Khmer language inscription dates from A.D. 611. Loti's idea of an Indian conquest is imaginative.

man—the powerful sovereigns of Angkor saw, arriving from the west, missionaries in yellow robes, bearers of the new light which amazed the Asiatic world. The Buddha, the predecessor of his brother Jesus, had achieved the enlightenment of India, and his emissaries were spreading over the Far East, to preach there that same morality of pity and love which the disciples of Christ had recently brought to Europe. Then the savage temples of Brahma became Buddhist temples; the statues of the altars changed their attitudes and lowered their eyes with gentler smiles.[6]

It would seem that under Buddhism the town of Angkor knew the apogee of its glory. But the history of its swift and mysterious decline has never been written, and the invading forest guards the secret of it. The little Cambodia of today, the repository and preserver of complicated rites the significance of which is no longer known, is a last remnant of that vast empire of the Khmers, which for more than five hundred years now has been extinguished under the silence of trees and mosses.[7]

Through the gloom, then, we approach the Gate of Victory, which at first seemed to us the entrance of a cave. It is surmounted, though, with monstrous representations of Brahma, which are hidden from us by the entwined roots, and on either

6. Mahayanist Buddhism probably appeared in Cambodia at the same time as Brahmanism, as part of the Indianization of the country. Most early rulers found in Brahmanism, more particularly in Shiva, a greater support for their authority. Jayavarman VII (reigned c. 1181–1219) was not a devotee of Shiva or Vishnu, but the Buddha of Mahayanism. Cambodia seems to have shifted to Theravadism decisively in the fifteenth century, though it was to be found in the country from the end of the thirteenth century. The peak of Angkor's power was probably under Suryavarman II (r.1113–1150). the builder of Angkor Wat, and a follower of Vishnu, not the Buddha.

7. The decline of Cambodia coincided with the rise of the Thai, and the final Siamese attack on Angkor in 1431 dealt the death blow to the great empire. Angkor was not entirely abandoned; it was briefly reoccupied by a Cambodian king Chan in the 1550s and 1560s. Loti's "more than five hundred years" is mild poetic licence.

side, in a kind of niche overhung by foliage, shapeless triple-headed elephants are concealed.[8]

Beyond this gate crowned with gloomy visages, we penetrate into what was once the immense town. You need to know this, for, within the walls, the forest continues, just as shady, and as dense, its age-old branches spreading out just as high. We get down from our carts at this point and advance on foot by pathways that are scarcely discernible, like tracks of wild beasts. For guide I have my Cambodian interpreter who is a regular frequenter of the ruins; and as I follow him the sound of our footsteps is smothered in the grasses and we hear only the quiet gliding of the snakes, the fleet flight of the monkeys.

Scarcely recognizable debris of architecture may be seen, however, on every side, mingled with and almost concealed by ferns, cycads, and orchids, by all that flora of the eternal twilight which flourishes here beneath the vault of the high trees. A number of Buddhist statues, some small, some of medium size, and some enormous, seated on thrones, are smiling at nothing. They had been hewn out of hard stone, and have remained, each in its place, after the collapse of the temples, which must have been made of carved wood. In almost every case pious pilgrims have made for them a roof of thatch as a shelter from the heavy storm showers; people have even burnt sticks of incense to them, and brought them flowers. But no monks dwell in their neighbourhood on account of the dreaded "fever of the woods," which makes it dangerous to sleep under the thickness of the green treetops, and even at the times of the great pilgrimages they are left to pass their nights in solitude.

Here were palaces once; here lived prodigiously ostentatious kings, of whom we now know nothing, who have passed into oblivion without leaving so much as a name graven on a stone or

8. Whilst the Hindu god Indra is seated on the central elephant (a representation of his mount Erewan) flanked by an apsara, the image over the gateway is the all-seeing bodhisattva of compassion, Avolekitesvara, which may be an anthropomorphic representation of the builder-king Jayavarman VII.

in someone's memory.[9] They have been built by men, these towering rocks, which are now at one with the forest, entwined by thousands of roots, clasped as in the tentacles of octopuses.

For there is an obstinacy for destruction even amongst the plants. The prince of death, called by the Brahmans Shiva, he who for each kind of animal has created the particular enemy which consumes it, for every creature its devouring microbes, seems to have foreseen in the darkness of the beginning of the world that men would try to perpetuate themselves a little by building things that might endure. And so, to annihilate their work, he conceived, amongst a thousand other agents of destruction, the pellitory plants, and, above all, the "fig-tree of the ruins"[10] which nothing is able to withstand.

The "fig-tree of the ruins" reigns today as undisputed master over Angkor. Above the palaces, above the temples, which it has patiently broken up, it flaunts everywhere in triumph its pale, smooth branches, spotted like a snake, and its large dome of leaves. At the beginning it was only a small seed, sown by the wind on a frieze or on the summit of a tower. But no sooner did it germinate than its roots, like tenuous filaments, insinuated their way between the stones, to go down, down, guided by a sure instinct, towards the earth. And when at last they reached the earth, they quickly swelled, waxing on its nourishing juices, until they became enormous, disjoining, displacing everything, splitting the thick walls from top to bottom; and then the building was irretrievably lost.

9. Loti was writing and publishing at a time when the enormous body of research undertaken by the Ecole Française d'Extrême Orient (EFEO), established in 1898, at the Conservation d'Angkor (founded 1907) had hardly begun. Many important inscriptions naming kings and their accomplishments have since been discovered, allowing the history of the Angkorean empire to be pieced together.

10. Loti is referring to the pernicious tree known in French as *fromager*, in English the bombax or silk-cotton tree. Its appearance has something of a fig-tree, but it is far larger and produces no edible fruit.

The forest, always the forest, and always its shadow, its sovereign oppression. One feels that it is hostile, murderous, that it breeds fever and death; and in the end one is seized with a desire to escape from its terrifying stranglehold. And then, suddenly, the occasional birds that were singing become silent; and what is this sudden darkeness? It is not late. There must be something more up there than the thickness of the overhanging greenery to make the pathways seem so dark. A general drumming on the leaves announces the advent of a tropical deluge. We had not seen that, above the trees, the sky had suddenly become black. The water streams down, pours in torrents upon our heads. Quickly, let us take refuge over there, near to that large, contemplative Buddha, in the shelter of his roof of thatch.

The involuntary hospitality of the god lasts a considerable time, and there is something inexpressibly sad in the mystery of the forest half-light, at the fading of the day.

When, at length, the deluge abates, it is time to leave the forest if we wish to avoid being overtaken by the night there. But we had almost reached the Bayon, the most ancient of the sanctuaries of Angkor, celebrated for its towers with four faces.[11] Through the semi-obscurity of the forest trees we can see it from here, looking like a chaotic heap of rocks. Let us risk going to see it.

Through an inextricable tangle of dripping brambles and creepers, we have to beat a path with sticks in order to reach this temple. The forest entwines it tightly on every side, chokes it,

11. The Bayon, built by Jayavarman VII at the end of the twelfth century, the most important Mahayanist Buddhist monument in Angkor, was in fact one of the last major temples built there. It was constructed in great haste, with several changes of plan, in the centre of the new city of Angkor Thom; undoubtedly its advanced ruinous state, caused in part by the haste with which it was erected, gave Loti to think it was the most ancient building in Angkor (Mouhot, writing half a century earlier, rightly considered Phnom Bakheng as the earliest). It has fifty-four towers, each with a face of the bodhisattva Avolekitesvara pointing to the cardinal directions.

crushes it; and to complete the destruction, immense "fig-trees of the ruins" have taken root there everywhere, up to the very summit of its towers, which act as their pedestal. Here are the doors; roots, like aged heads of hair, drape them with a thousand fringes; at this already late hour in the obscurity which descends from the trees and the rain-charged sky, they are deep, dark holes, which make one pause. From the nearest entrance, some monkeys which had come there for shelter, and were sitting in a circle as if for some council, make their escape, without haste and without any noise; it seems that in this place silence is imposed upon everything. We hear only the furtive sound of the water as it drips from the foliage and stones after the shower.

My Cambodian guide insists that we should leave. We have no lanterns, he tells me, on our carts, and we must return before the hour of the tiger. So be it, let us go. But we shall return just for this infinitely mysterious temple.

Before I leave, however, I raise my eyes to look at the towers which overhang me, drowned in verdure, and I shudder suddenly with an indefinable fear as I perceive, falling upon me from above, a huge, fixed smile; and then another smile again, beyond, on another stretch of wall; then three, then five, then ten. They appear everywhere, and I realize that I have been overlooked from all sides by the four-faced towers. I had forgotten them, although I had been warned about them. These masks carved in the air are so far exceeding human proportions that it requires a moment or two fully to comprehend them. They smile under their great flat noses, and half close their eyelids, with an indescribable air of senile femininity, looking like aged, discreetly cunning ladies. They are likenesses of the gods worshipped, in times obliterated, by those men whose history is now unknown; likenesses from which, over centuries, neither the slow labour of the forest nor the heavy dissolving rains have been able to remove the *expression*, the ironical good humour, which is more disquieting than the rictus of the monsters of China.

Our oxen trot smartly on the return journey, as if they, too, realized that it was necessary to escape before nightfall from this soaked and steaming forest, which now becomes dark almost immediately, without any interval of twilight. And the memory of those over-large old ladies who are smiling discreetly over there behind us, above the heaps of ruins, continues to pursue me throughout the course of our jolting, bumpy flight through the jungle.

When at length I reach the open air again, before the broad moats of water lilies at the entrance to the Cyclopean bridge, the clear-swept sky has assumed a crystal-like limpidity, and it is the moment when the stars begin to pulse. At the end of the clearing which now reappears, the towers of the temple of Angkor Wat rise up very high. They are no longer, as at midday, pale and almost nebulous from the excess of sunlight; they are now stamped out vividly clear against the background of greenish gold, with the silhouettes of their muliple-banded tiaras; and a large star, one of the first to light up, shines above, magnificently. Then there comes back to me, like a refrain, the childish phrase of long ago: "In the depths of the forests of Siam, I have seen the evening star rise over the great ruins of Angkor."

After the stifling vaults of trees, after the forest full of ambushes, one gets at once a feeling of security, a sense of being at home, on returning to the immense enclosure of the temple, where the bushes are scarcely taller than a man, and the paved causeway goes straight and sure towards a semblance of a village. The chanting of the monks is also there to welcome me, and when I climb by the little ladder into my dwelling on piles and without walls, everything seems hospitable.

IT is in the dead of night, preceded by a Siamese torch-bearer, that I cross at last the threshold of the colossal temple of Angkor Wat. It had been my original intention not to begin the pilgrimage before tomorrow at daybreak; but it is there, so close, almost overhanging its frightening mass above my frail lodging.

Up a few granite steps and I am in a first gallery of prodigious length, which has the intimidating sonority and seemed at first to have the silence of a cave; but which is immediately filled with rustling sounds.

This is the exterior gallery, which forms a square, each side some two hundred and fifty metres long,[12] and surrounds, like a sumptuous rampart path, the jumbled terraces of the central structures. Its flagstones are carpeted with something soft which yields to our footsteps, giving off a mingled odour of musk and dung. And to the rustling which greeted our arrival are now added little piercing cries, which spread before us into the obscure distances.

As we pass, our torch reveals, on the sombre grey walls, an inextricable confusion of warriors gesticulating furiously; along the whole length of the gallery, an uninterrupted bas-relief stretches as far as one can see its battles, combatants in thousands, caparisoned elephants, monsters, and war chariots. I have no intention of venturing tonight into the dangerous labyrinth of the centre, into the temple proper, but I should like to go around the outer galleries, which are so straight and look so easy, and to continue to follow to the end the story of the bas-relief. But I am troubled by these little piercing cries above my head, which are multiplied in concert, as if uttered by thousands of rats. And then, high up, instead of stones of the vault, does it not seem that there is a quivering of black cloth? Oh! The adorable creatures carved here and there upon the walls, as if to afford a respite to the eyes from the long battle: holding in their hand a lotus flower, they stand two by two, or three by three, calm and smiling beneath their archaic tiaras. They are the divine Apsaras[13] of the Hindu theogonies. How lovingly the artists of old have chiselled and polished their virginal breasts! What has become of the dust of the beauties from whom their perfect bodies were copied? Goodness gracious: now the vault is sinking towards us, or at least the quivering black cloth objects which seem to be suspended from it are. They come down to touch our

12. It is actually rectangular, 215 by 187 metres.

13. Celestial maidens, dancers and courtesans, the perfection of beauty.

hair; we can feel the wind they make like a vigorous fanning. Hairy bodies very rapidly moving long hairless membranes. It was these, then, that uttered those cries above, like so many rats. We are brushed on all sides by enormous bats, in a cloud, in an avalanche, maddened, aggressive! They are going to put out our wan little light. Every man for himself! Let us make for the doors; this temple obviously ought not to be profaned in the solemn hours of the night.

Outside, sudden peace, serenity of sky, and starlit splendour. We stop in our flight to inhale deliciously; the air is fragrant with jasmine, and the tranquil psalmody of the monks, after those multitudinous cries in our ears, seems an exquisite music. All those tortured figures which peopled the walls, and all those touchings by horrible wings. From what hideous nightmare have we escaped!

Moreover, it is the enchanted hour of these regions, the hour when the brazier of the sun is extinguished, and the evil dew has not begun to moisten everything. In the immense clearing defended by moats and walls, in the middle of which the temple sits in state, one has a feeling of complete security, notwithstanding the surroundings and the great forests. Tigers do not cross the stone bridges, although now the gates are never shut, and, excepting some curious monkeys, all the beasts of the forests respect the enclosed park where men dwell and sing.

And the long causeway is there, stretching straight and safe before me, whitish in the night, between the dark tufts of the bushes scented with jasmine and tuberose. Aimlessly I begin to wander slowly over its flagstones, moving further away from the temple, hearing less and less distinctly the song of the monks, which by degrees dies away behind me in the infinite silence.

I walked on and on until I reached the lotus-covered moat, with its exit bridge guarded by the seven-headed serpents. On the further bank the forest spreads its high black curtain; it draws me to it, with its air of sleep and mystery. Without entering it, what if I went just as far as the edge of its benighted trees, where so many attentive ears must already have heard me. And cautiously

I pass through the portico, making sure of each stone on which I tentatively set my foot; in such darkness as this, to cross the bridge inspires respect.

But I seem to hear light footsteps running towards me from behind. Men or monkeys? And before I have time to turn round I feel myself taken by the hand, so very gently, and two human shapes appear, who seek to detain me. I recognize them at once—they are two of my worthy Siamese drovers. What do they want with me? To understand one another we have not a single word of any language in common. But they indicate to me by signs that it is foolhardy to proceed further; there are ambushes out there, and there are beasts with teeth that bite. I let them have their way and lead me back.

They bring me to a chosen spot where some other simple drovers, also of my company, are stretched smoking cigarettes and enjoying the cool air. It is on the wide, low rampart wall, which forms a terrace above the defensive moats. It seems that I am expected to lie down too. To do so on the earth would be impossible on account of the numerous sly, poisonous things which crawl in the grass; but on the old polished flagstones there is no kind of risk. One of the drovers takes off the thin garment which covered his copper-coloured torso, and rolling it into a ball, makes a pillow for my head; after which I must smoke one of their cigarettes which exhales a strangely pleasant and soothing odour of burning grass. We cannot talk to one another, of course, but—no doubt because silence here has in it something intimidating—one of the young drovers intones very softly in falsetto a little lullaby which sounds like the lament of some spirit of the ruins; merely to hear it makes me feel that I have wandered far, into a country at once unknown and incomprehensible. And the constellations, too, which above my upturned head shine in the blue-black of the infinite, give to me in their own way a permanent signal of exile. The Great Bear, which is throned on high in our nights in France, seems to have slipped down the sky and has almost disappeared below the horizon;

while, on the opposite side, I see shining, very clearly, the Southern Cross.

It was at first a delicious sensation to recline in this way, half-naked, confident of the equable and caressing warmth of an atmosphere which cannot ever at any time turn cold, and in which one knows that there will never rise a rough breeze. But the moments of well-being in these regions are numbered; around us a slight humming sound, faint to begin with, swells minute by minute, and becomes general: the mosquitoes are assembling, having scented from a distance the unwonted odour of flesh. And already, too, the linen with which I am clothed begins to soften and draws in the humidity. The eternal moisture of these regions, which had called a truce for an hour or two, reappears now in the form of dew. We are sprinkled with tiny drops of water, and we must seek shelter at the foot of the great temple, in the hamlet of the chanting monks, beneath the pilgrims' shed.

It is under this shed, protected by its little altar to Buddha, that I prepare at last to sleep. The piles lift me above the ground where poisonous beasts crawl, and an outspread curtain of muslin is my protection against the beasts that fly. Around me the yellow drovers in my party install themselves, and as they have no mosquito nets, they arrange to take turns until the morning in maintaining, beneath the open-work flooring of our lodging, a large fire of grasses, which will envelop us all in a protecting cloud. And, lulled by the Buddhist chanting, I soon fall into a deep sleep, in the midst of an odorous smoke.

CHAPTER VIII

Friday, 29th November 1901.

AWAKENED at dawn by the morning crescendo of the chanting. There has been such an excess of humidity during the night, so heavy a dew, that in spite of the thatched roof everything around me and on me is soaked, as after a shower.

In the comparative freshness of the early morning, I again climb the first steps of the temple, between the worn balustrades, defaced by the rains of centuries. And, mindful of the guardian bats, I enter with an excess of caution, making no more noise than a cat. My enemies of last night are all asleep above, hanging, head downwards, by their claws from the stones overhead and simulating at this hour myriads of dark velvet little bags. I have entered now, and none of them has so much as moved. I recognize the gallery, with its cave-like resonance, which is decorated as far as eye can see with the endless bas-relief of battles. And now that I see it in its entirety, diminishing before me in unbroken perspective, it seems even more infinitely long. A green half-light has replaced all at once the clear daylight that was dawning outside. There is a smell of dampness, like that encountered in basements, but it is dominated here by the fusty musk-scented odour of the excrement of the bats, which is deposited in a layer upon the ground as if a rain of brown grains fell constantly from the vault.

To illumine the unfolding of the bas-relief, which covers all the interior wall of the gallery, windows at intervals open on to the surrounding copse, and admit an attenuated light, made green by the foliage and palms. Very sumptuous windows, too, framed with carvings so delicate that one might think lace had been overlaid on the stone. They have ringed bars, which look like little columns of wood, elaborately turned by lathe, but are, in fact, of sandstone, like the rest of the walls.

This bas-relief, which stretches its tussle of characters over a kilometre[1] on the four sides of the temple, is inspired by one of the most ancient epics conceived by the men of Asia, those Aryans who were our ancestors.

"Formerly, in the age called Kuta, lived the sons of Kyacyapa, who were of superhuman strength and beauty. They had been born of two sisters, Diti and Aditi. But the sons of Aditi were gods, while the sons of Diti were demons.

"One day when they were all assembled in council to discover a means by which they might escape old age and death, they decided to gather all those plants of the woods which are called simples, to cast them into the sea of milk and then to churn the sea. There would result from this a magic liquor which would conquer death and make them strong and beautiful for ever.

"Accordingly they made a churn with a mountain, and a cord with the great holy serpent Vasuki, and began to churn unceasingly.

"Presently, from the swirling waters, arose the Apsaras, celestial dancers and courtesans, who were of incomparable beauty. They became the wives of the demi-gods, the Gandharwas, and gave birth to the race of monkeys.

"Then there appeared in person the beautiful Varuni, daughter of the Ocean, whom the sons of Aditi took for their wife. Finally,

1. This is a slight exaggeration: including the four corner pavilions, the carvings of the four sides of the gallery, two metres high, comprise 1,200 square metres of sandstone bas-reliefs. Most—the best—date from the twelfth century, but those on the sides forming the northeast corner were carved in the sixteenth.

on the surface of the sea they saw forming the marvellous liquor which was to triumph over death. But to possess it, a war of extermination began between the sons of Diti and the sons of Aditi, and the sons of Aditi conquered."

Such in summary is the theme of the Ramayana, that ancestral legend which has come down to us thanks to the labours of the pious Valmiki, the holy mountain hermit who in primeval times took pains to transcribe and perpetuate it in a poem of twenty-five thousand verses.[2]

The churning of the sea of milk[3] alone fills a panel more than fifty metres long. Then come the battles of the gods and demons[4] and those of the monkeys against the evil spirits[5] of the Island of Ceylon, who had seized the beautiful Sita, the spouse of Rama.

All these pictures, which formerly were painted and gilded, have taken on, under the seeping of the eternal humidity, a sad blackish colour, varied in places by glistenings of actual wetness. Moreover, the bas-relief, which measures five metres in height,[6] is worn, as high as a man can reach, by the secular friction of fingers—for in the times of pilgrimage the whole multitude makes it a duty to touch it. Here and there, in the parts illuminated by the beautiful windows with their carved bars, one can still see traces of colouring on the robes or faces; and sometimes in the tiaras of the Apsaras, a little gold, spared by time, continues to shine. As I advance I do not cease to watch out for the velvety guardians above; the flagstones sound hollow and when my footsteps make too much a noise, some pairs of

2. Valmiki is credited with the authorship in the Vedic or earliest known period of both the Ramayana and the Mahabharata, epics of Indian origin with widespread currency in Southeast Asia. The source of Loti's text has not been identified. Loti in his Journal only makes reference to the Ramayana as a source of inspiration for the bas-reliefs. In his subsequent reworking of this basic material, he read up on his subject.

3. On the southern section of the east gallery, one of the best preserved.

4. On the western side of the north gallery.

5. On the west gallery.

6. An exaggeration: two metres.

hairless membranes unfold; a bat stretches itself, wakes another one, and a general stirring ensues. Then I stand quite still, as if turned to stone, until all are asleep again.

What is difficult to understand is that the wall with all its people seems to be in a single piece over a length of some hundreds of metres; it needs a close scrutiny to detect the joints of the enormous stones which have been placed together in line without the help of any cement, and adjusted with the same rigorous precision as in the monuments of Egyptian antiquity.

In the middle of each side of the quadrilateral, a portico opens from this outer gallery and gives access to the central court, where rises the temple proper, the prodigious mass of sculptured sandstone scaling the blue sky. Into that I hesitate to penetrate, intimidated, perhaps, or wearied in advance by such a jumble of stairways, terraces, and towers, by such a complication of lines, by the heavy mass of the silent whole. Rather than enter, I continue to loiter, following the bas-relief of the outer gallery.

In the gallery on the fourth side I encounter two young novices, clothed in lemon-yellow and orange-yellow robes. What are they doing here with a wheelbarrow, a shovel, and a broom? Nothing more nor less than gathering the bats' dung to manure some little monastic garden. I wonder how many thousands of millions of insects, eaten in the air, are represented by these heaps of brown grains in their wheelbarrow, which are on the way now to fertilize flowers, which will nourish other insects, which will be eaten by other bats!

But they are making too much noise, these young monks—although in truth they make scarcely any—for, above, the velvety sleepers are awakening.

To avoid their bold wings, I rush hastily through one of the porticoes into the central courtyard. And thus, after having lingered for a long time around the tangled chaos of the sanctuaries, I abruptly enter it at last in a dash to escape.

It is at a moment when the light all at once becomes overcast, as if the sun were passing through some great eclipse. Above the masses of terraces, porticoes and stairways, entangled with prodigal verdure, the clouds have suddenly spread a vault of darkness; a torrent of rain is about to pour upon the ruins. And all the beasts which dwell there under the leaves and in the holes in the walls become silent, attentive to what is about to fall.

This temple is one of the places in the world where men have heaped together the greatest mass of stones, where they have accumulated the greatest wealth of sculptures, of ornaments, of foliated scrolls, of flowers, and of faces. It is not simple as are the clean lines of Thebes and Baalbek.[7] Its complexity is bewildering as well as its enormity. Monsters guard all the flights of steps, all the entrances; the divine Apsaras, in indefinitely repeated groups, are seen everywhere amongst the overhanging creepers. And, at a first sight, nothing stands out; there seem only disorder and confusion in this hill of carved stone blocks, on the summit of which the great towers have sprouted.

But, on the contrary, when one examines it a little, a perfect symmetry becomes clear from top to bottom. The hill of sculptured stones forms a square pyramid with three levels, the base measuring more than a kilometre in circumference; and it is on the third and highest of these levels will be found, no doubt, what is the pre-eminently holy place. I have to climb, therefore—I was prepared for it—to climb by steep and uneven steps, between the smiling Apsaras, the crouching lions, the holy serpents spreading like a fan their seven heads, and the languid verdure, which at this moment is motionless in the still air; to climb in haste, too, so as to reach the top before the deluge begins. In coming here this morning, I had imagined that the ascent would be made under a blue sky and in the glare of the sun, breezes stirring the branches, and everywhere around the sounds of birds, insects, and reptiles fleeing at my approach. But this mournful stillness daunts me; I was not prepared for this silence of waiting nor for this black sky. No, my arrival wakens

7. Thebes, the ancient city of upper Egypt on the Nile, with its monuments of the twelfth dynasty (c. 2052–1786 B.C.); Baalbek in Lebanon, with its Roman monuments of the first to third centuries A.D.

not a single sound, not a single movement, and even the sing-song of the monks, as they chant without ceasing at the foot of the temple, reaches me only very faintly, from the distance.

Now I have reached the first of the three platforms. Before me rises the second level of a *height double that of the first*, presenting stairways more abrupt, more guarded by smiles and the rictus of stone. It is surrounded on its four sides by a vaulted gallery, a kind of cloister, immense and pompously magnificent, with its excess of carvings, its porticoes crowned with a surfeit of strange lintels, with its narrow windows, the sandstone bars of which, already too massive, are brought close together as if the better to imprison you. All around the dilapidation is extreme. Within, the decoration is simpler than in the corridors of the base. The place is damp and dark, and there is an intolerable odour of bats; they cover the vault, these suspended sleepers. At this height I no longer hear anything of the litany of the monks, and the silence is so profound that one scarcely dares to walk.

The second platform is surrounded like the first by its cloister, the facades of which are wrought with as much elaboration as the most patient embroideries. Here the visitor might reasonably think that he was nearly there; but now the third level rises, *of a height double that of the second*, and the monumental stairway that leads up to it, with its worn, grass-grown steps, is so steep that it induces vertigo. The gods desire, no doubt, to make themselves more inaccessible in proportion as one tries to approach them. Indeed, the temple seems to grow higher, to stretch out, to reach up towards the dark sky, and it is a little like those exhausting dreams in which we strive madly to reach a goal which flies before us. There should be four of these staircases, watched over by Apsaras, one on each of the sides of the enormous pedestal; but I have not time to choose the best, for the shadow of the clouds grows ever deeper, and the drenching is at hand. I go up almost running, and the forest, the sovereign forest, seems to rise at the same time; on every side it begins to stretch its circle to the horizon like a sea.

The third square platform is bordered also with its cloister, the facades of which are carved even more magnificently. In high relief on the walls are the inevitable Apsaras standing in groups, and welcoming me with smiles of quiet mockery, eyes half-closed. On this topmost terrace, where I reach the bases of the great towers, and the very doors of the sanctuary, I must be more than thirty metres above the level of the plains.[8] And here the illusion is reversed. It seems now that it is the temple which has sunk into the forest. Seen from here it looks as though it is submerged, buried in the middle of the greenery. Below me, three graduated courses of cloisters, of high-crowned porticoes, of sumptuous vaults, hardly touched by the centuries, have plunged, as it were, into the trees, into the silent expanse of trees, the tops of which, in the distance, and as far as eye can see, simulate the undulation of an ocean swell.

The rain! A few first drops, astonishingly large and heavy, by way of warning. And then almost at once the general drumming on the leaves, torrents of water which descend in fury. Then, through a portico, the overloaded lintel of which is in the form of flames and finials, running to take shelter, I enter at last what must be the sanctuary itself.

I expected the immense hall, where I should be alone, whereas it is only another gallery, infinitely long but narrow, oppressive, sinister, in which I shudder almost at meeting, in the half-light of the storm and the excessively barred windows, a number of motionless people—people eaten by worms, corpses and phantoms of gods, seated or propped along the walls.

The majority are of human stature, but some are gigantic, and others are dwarfs. Some are of a dull grey, others of a blood-coloured red, and here and there a little gilding, as in the masks of mummies, still shines on some of the faces. Many are without hands, without arms, without heads, and a mass of bats' excrement humps their backs, deforms their shoulders. And

8. The base of the third level is 13 metres high and the whole rises 40 metres above the second level. The base of the quincunx of sanctuary towers is 42 metres above the upper level.

when I raise my eyes, how the sight fills me with disgust! For here, more even than below, the stone ceilings are covered with these little velvet pouches which hang suspended by their claws, and want but the slightest noise to unfold and become a whirlwind of wings. Internally, the thick, blackish walls, lacking any decoration, are half concealed by fine draperies, like mourning veils, which are the work of innumerable spiders. Outside rages the noise of the downpour. Everything is inundated; the water streams down in cascades. I breathe a warm vapour at once fetid and musk-scented. In the long gallery the closeness of the walls and the enormous size of the sandstone spindles which mask the openings make one feel too confined; yet the circle of the horizon, seen between these window bars, supports the notion of altitude, serves as a reminder that one dominates, from the height of this kind of aerial prison, the infinite expanse of the sodden forest.

This, then, is the sanctuary which formerly haunted my childish imagination, which I have only at last reached after many journeyings about the world, in what is already the evening of my wandering life. It gives me a mournful welcome. I had not foreseen these torrents of rain, this confinement amongst the spiders' webs, nor my present solitude in the midst of so many phantom gods. There is above all one personage over there, reddish like a flayed corpse, with worm-eaten and crumbling feet, who, in order that he may not fall altogether, leans crosswise against the wall, half-upturning his face with its pitted lips. It is from him, it seems, that all the silence and all the unutterable sadness of the place proceed.

A prisoner here for as long as the storm may last, I go first of all to a window, instinctively, to get more air, to escape the odour of the bats. And between the rigid spindle-shaped bars, I see falling away from me the architectural mass which I have just climbed. On the sides of the ruins, all the foliage bends and trembles, overwhelmed by the tumultuous downpour. The legions of Apsaras, the great holy serpents, the monsters crouching on the thresholds of the flights of steps, seem to bow their heads under the daily deluge, which, for seasons without number, has worn them away by constantly washing them. The water can be heard crackling more and more, rushing in a thousand streams.

In order to discern the general plan of this third and highest platform, it would be necessary to see it from outside. But the light continues to fade as if it were the twilight instead of the morning; the horizon of the forests is completely hidden behind the ever more opaque curtains of the rain, and it is clear that the storm will last for another hour at least. I have out of necessity to remain in this shelter, and in this persistent half-light of eclipse. Feeling that I am followed by the cadaverous smiles of all this assembly of Buddhas who are watching me, I proceed towards what must be the centre and very heart of Angkor Wat.

I tread softly on the layers of dust and excrement, sprinkled with feathers of owls. The huge, hairy spiders, weavers of the multiple draperies, remain motionless and on watch.

Over and above that which falls unceasingly from the roof, little heaps of withered flowers and incense appear before all the statues, proving that they are still worshipped. But why do not people dust them a little when they come to visit them? And in what disorder, too, they have been left! The small, the large, and the colossal, all jumbled up as after a disorderly retreat. At the uncertain date of the sack of the town and the pillage of the temple they must all have been overthrown and laid flat. Subsequently the piety of the Siamese put them upright again, as best they could, but grouping them anyhow along the walls, those of hard sandstone against those of worm-eaten wood, which crumble to powder at the slightest touch, those which have lost their colouring besides those which still possess red robes and gilded faces. (And, lest they should forget a single one of them in their devotions, the pilgrims who come here spend hours, it seems, in passing through the endless galleries where they repose.) Buddhist statues, already many times centenarian, they were yet newcomers, quite recent intruders in this temple of a far more ancient cult. But having supplanted the images of

Brahma, the primitive god of Angkor,[9] they are now fallen in their turn, destroyed by time.

The flagstones are so carpeted with filth and ashes that the sound of my footsteps is smothered, and, without being heard by the thousands of little ears above, I can make my way towards the darker end of the gallery, between the two rows of silent personages. Here, formerly, was the Holy of Holies, the place where the supreme Brahma was enthroned; but it has been walled up at an unknown period of time.[10]

And in front of this wall—which, no doubt, still encloses the terrible statue and perhaps preserves it as intact as a mummy in its sarcophagus—a Buddha of gigantic size, commanding and gentle, has been seated for centuries, with legs crossed and downcast half-closed eyes, for so many centuries that the spiders have contrived patiently to drape him with black muslins, hiding his gilding, and the bats have had time to cover him as with a thick mantle of droppings. The swarm of horrible little sleeping beasts now form a kind of padded canopy of brown plush above his head, and the rain, which continues to stream down mercilessly outside, makes its plaintive daily music for him. But his bowed head, which I can distinguish in spite of the darkness, preserves the same smile as may be found on all representations of him, from Tibet to China: the smile of the Great Peace, obtained by the Great Renunciation and the Great Pity.

IN the evening, as I once more ascend to the temple, after having

9. As mentioned in note 6 on page 35, Suryavarman II, the builder of Angkor Wat, followed the cult of Vishnu rather than, more generally, Brahma.

10. The doorways to the central shrine in Angkor Wat were walled up some time after the sack of Angkor by the Siamese. They were opened up by the French archaeologist Jean Commaille, keeper of the monuments in Angkor from 1907 to 1916. A vertical shaft 27 m deep with the temple foundation deposit was discovered at the very centre of the monument. The approaches to the central shrine became a depot for the late (post-twelfth century) Buddha statues.

slept below, at its foot, in the pilgrim shed during the heat of the day, one would never believe that it had rained in torrents all the morning. The sky is of a splendrous blue that seems immutable. The earth has quickly drunk up the excessive water, and the burning sun has dried the trees of the forest and the verdure which clings to the ruins. All is luminous, calm, and hot, much more so than in the finest of our summer days. The Apsaras, the monsters, the half-effaced bas-reliefs, the masses of immense dead stones, are bathed now in a sort of ironical and mournful magnificence. And the thousands of little invaders of the sanctuary, those which fly, those which run, and those which crawl, have emerged from their hiding-places of the morning, and begun again to plunder. All around can be heard the rustling of serpents and lizards, the singing of turtle-doves and little birds, the miaowing of wild cats. Large butterflies, like cut-outs of precious silks, career about, and myriads of flies, in corslets of velvet or golden green, mingle with the psalmody of the monks their murmuring like the distant ringing of bells. The bats alone, the importunate bats, prime masters of Angkor Wat, sleep on in perpetual shadow, glued to the vaults of the cloisters.

With time and neglect each of the superposed terraces of the temple has become a kind of suspended garden where the immense leaves of the banana trees are mingled with the white tufts of a most fragrant jasmine flowering in bunches. All this, and a thousand other exotic plants and the tall wild grasses, all this after seeming to die beneath the lashing of the rain, has risen again more vigorous than before, and with a freshness more sparkling amidst the decrepitude of the stones.

Without hurrying this time, for no cloud threatens me, I climb the arduous steps which lead, above, to the dwelling of the gods. Oh, the graceful and exquisite carvings scattered in profusion everywhere! These ornamental scrolls, this leaf-work and decorative foliage—how to explain it—resemble those which appeared in France in the time of François I and the Medicis.[11]

For a moment one might be tempted to believe, if it were not an impossiblity, that the artists of our Renaissance had sought their models on these walls, which, nevertheless, in their days had been slumbering for three or four centuries, in the midst of forests, quite unsuspected by Europe.

I climb without haste, lit by a glaring and deathly sun, and along my difficult uphill path a multitude of intimidating symbols is spaced out. Everywhere monsters, and combats of monsters. Everywhere the sacred Naga, trailing over the balustrades its long, undulating body, and then rearing its seven viperish heads to frighten people away. The Apsaras, how pretty and smiling they are, in their coiffures of goddesses, with, nevertheless, always that expression of mysteriously hinting at something which is so disturbing. Richly adorned, with bracelets, necklaces, headbands of precious stones, tall tiaras, either pointed or surmounted by a tuft of plumes, they hold between their delicate fingers sometimes a lotus flower, and sometimes an enigmatic emblem. All of those which can be reached in passing have been so often caressed in the course of centuries that their beautiful bare bosoms shine as under a varnish. For the women who come here during the pilgrimages touch them passionately in order that they may obtain from them the grace to become mothers. In their niches embroidered with carvings, they remain adorable. But what a pity that their feet should so disfigure them! They are always enormous, as in the bas-reliefs of Egypt, and always drawn in profile, whilst the legs face you fully. But they also occasion considered reflection, too, in these ineptly drawn feet, for they remind us that the fair goddesses are the work of a very primitive humanity, which in its art was still battling with

11. François I (1494–1547), King of France from 1515, was a patron of the arts and under him the French Renaissance reached its height. The Medici family played an important part in the cultural history of Florence, especially in the fifteenth and sixteenth centuries. Catherine de Medici (1519–1589) was the influential queen of Henri II, François I's successor.

the difficulties of draughtsmanship, still baffled by the mystery of foreshortening.[12]

One other thing of which they were ignorant, those proud architects of Angkor Wat, and that is the large expanded vault. Their ancestors had taught them only what can be obtained by corbelling, and which must necessarily remain narrow and heavy. That is why all the galleries they managed to build are suffocating, why they superposed cloisters upon cloisters, created massive terraces, heaped blocks on top of blocks. And this temple, no doubt, with that of the Bayon, which has subsided into the neighbouring forest, is the most massive mountain of stones that men have dared to undertake since the pyramids of Memphis.[13]

As each level is reached, there is a momentary respite of shade, in the hot humidity of the bordering cloister.

But a sun of fire beats down on the last staircase, which is twice as high as the preceding one, and the steepest of all, leading to the topmost platform which seems to climb into the sky. In truth, this progressive doubling of the height, from one level to another, is an architectural discovery for increasing the size of the temple by creating an illusion which is impossible to escape. I experience it this evening as I experienced it this morning under the dark rain-clouds: it is as if the dwelling of the gods, as you approach it, flies before you, soaring into the air.

The successive reduction of the internal decoration as one approaches the Holy of Holies is deliberate, too, and is religious in a very effective way. I had already remarked on the use of similar means in the Brahmanistic temples of India, more

12. Loti was a competent amateur artist, and was rightly struck by the contrast between the elegance of the upper bodies of the apsara and the crudity of their gigantic sideways-facing feet.

13. The lack of a true arch (and the occasional recourse to wood to cover large openings) was indeed a constraint in Khmer architecture. Loti never visited Borobudur in Java and so could make no comparison in monumental size. Memphis, just south of Cairo, the Egyptian capital from c.3100–c.2100 B.C., he visited in 1894; he went again to Egypt in 1907.

particularly in those of Ellora,[14] where after a surfeit of sculpture in the lower galleries, the supreme symbol is found at last at the end of a grim hall with thick bare walls: the place where the divine symbol dwells should contain nothing that might distract the visitors from adoration and awe.

Arriving again in the last of the successive terraces, I enter a gallery of phantom statues, similar to that in which I took refuge during the storm, which leads in the darkness to a doorway blocked with stones, in front of which is again a large Buddha, very gentle in aspect, keeping vigil. *But this is not the same gallery as I was in this morning.* I do not recognize the wasted faces of the personages who inhabit it, and, besides, I have come to it by different staircases, through different porticoes.

It is now about five o'clock, and the golden rays of the sun are tinged a little with the red of the evening. No trace at all of the deluge of the morning. I now realize that, on this platform at the summit, there are four identical galleries, equally long, equally populous with funereal hosts, hung with the same black spiders' webs, and padded on the ceiling with the same sleeping bats. These four galleries form a cross with equal arms and meet at the Holy of Holies, which marks the centre of the temple-mountain.[15] But, after the extreme prodigality of ornamentation in the cloisters below, these highest naves, richly embellished as they are on the outside, disclose, in the interior, only square rough-hewn pillars, and uneven and defaced walls. It is because one should enter here only for prayer, having freed the spirit from all the mirages of this world. They were the thresholds of the Invisible and the Inexpressible, and nothing was needed here that might recall our vanities, our earthly luxuries. And in their

14. Loti visited the cave-temples of Ellora, in western India, in his journey through the sub-continent in the winter of 1899–1900, written up as *L'Inde (Sans les Anglais) (India, without the English)*, published in 1903.

15. Many Khmer temples were indeed a visual representation on earth of Mount Meru, the abode of the Hindu gods, and Loti's use of the term 'temple-mountain' is correct.

dark depths, behind the identical giant Buddhas, their identical doorways, which today are sealed, close off the four sides of the supreme retreat where, perhaps, the soul of the old temple subsists still, buried with the four terrible Brahmas.[16]

One of those colossal towers, in outline like a tiara, which can be seen so far away in the plain, rises at the end of each arm of the cross formed by the four naves, and, above the Holy of Holies where the naves meet, a fifth tower, the most astonishing and the most elaborate, surpassing all the others, commands from a height of some seventy metres the thick, green shroud of the forest. According to a learned Chinese writer, who visited this mysterious empire on the eve of its decline, about the thirteenth century,[17] and has left us the only known documents concerning its magnificence, this central tower was crowned with a golden lotus, so large that its sacred flower could be seen shining in the air from every point of the town, which today lies buried.

In the forest which surrounds me, and is revealed, under this pure evening sky, clear and distinct to the edge of the horizon, I had not noticed this morning a number of deciduous trees here and there, which are turning yellow, and shedding their leaves,

16. The Hindu trimurti comprises Brahma, Vishnu and Shiva. In Chapter VII Loti had already (wrongly) identified the image over the southern gate as that of Brahma, though he does not at that point mention its replication to face the four cardinal points. In Chapter IX he specifically identifies (again wrongly) the four faces of each of the towers of the Bayon with Brahma, hence the reference to 'four Brahmas' here. The original English translation discreetly omitted the word 'four'.

17. Chou Ta-kuan (Zhou Daguan) who spent nearly a year in Angkor from 1296–1297 as part of a Chinese embassy in the reign of Indravarman III (r.1295–1308). His account, published as *The Customs of Cambodia* in English, is invaluable for its details of daily life in the Khmer empire when past its prime. Loti probably consulted Paul Pelliot's translation, published in 1902. The Golden Tower mentioned by Chou Ta-kuan, in describing the walled city "flanked by more than twenty lesser towers and several hundred stone chambers" was probably the central tower of the Bayon, and not Angkor Wat, which lay outside the city.

because December is at hand. It reminds me that to come here I have, in fact, journeyed northwards for three or four days, and that already the country is not absolutely one of perpetual greenness, as was the Cochin-China from where I came. And in spite of the powerful, tranquil heat, an unexpected impression of autumn, of falling leaves, as in our forests, comes to augment for me all at once the nameless melancholy of these ruins.

I thought I should be alone to wander till nightfall in these high galleries. But, while I am watching, between the massive bars of a window, the sun, which before disappearing is setting everything on fire, some visitors, old grey-bearded men, arrive behind me, with timid, hushed steps. Their costumes show them to be pilgrims from Burma. Before each Buddha they make a salutation, deposit a flower, and light a stick of incense. Even to the most shapeless remains littering the floor, they pay their respects in passing, and whenever the remnant is in any way recognizable, an arm, a worm-eaten trunk, a head without a body, they stop and plant close by, between the joints of the paving, one of their burning sticks. And so once more the dead and musty air in which these images and these remains are achieving their return to dust is filled for a moment with a suave fragrance.

One of the pilgrims, however, the leader of the group, whispers something which seems to signify, "Let us hurry, night is approaching and will overtake us in the ruins." So they curtail their devotions, their marks of respect become briefer. Arriving before the Great Buddha, who, at the end of the gallery, guards the immured sanctuary, they select those places where the gilding of his legs is most faded, and carefully apply to them sheets of gold leaf which they extract from a wallet.[18] Then they depart. I hear the sound of their discreet footsteps die away as they descend the steep stone staircases.

18. Placing gold leaf on a Buddha statue is still a standard way of expressing respect for the image, and also of obtaining merit.

Their departure has suddenly made the solitude more imposing, and seems to make the daylight fade more quickly. Moreover the setting of the sun is so vertical and so rapid in these regions, which are almost without twilight!

Below me, the darkness has already encroached upon the architectural mass of which I have now a bird's-eye view, and also upon the expanse of the surrounding forest, where soon will open the innumerable eyes of the nocturnal beasts. Alone, two towers, which rise up in my vicinity, are still resplendent like glowing embers; the reddened rays light up, as in apotheosis, their unknown architecture, which is neither Hindu nor Chinese, which resembles that of no other country on the earth. If the ornamentation of the walls, the decorative foliage and leaf-work recalled our European Renaissance, these towers, on the contrary, are strikingly strange—the conception of a race apart, which gave a bright flash of light in this corner of the world, and then disappeared never to return. They rather resemble sheaves of organ-pipes, above which have been placed, at their various heights, papal crowns. Apsaras are to be found there too, along with very strangely haloed gods, and groups of monsters. In the sky, which is now changing and turning to the grey of dusk, they continue to glow for a few seconds longer, looking like metal reddened by fire, like the burning towers of goodness knows what magic palace.

Formerly in place of this sea of verdure, silent at my feet, the town of Angkor Thom (Angkor the Great) spread for some distance about the plain; and if we could now lop off the bushy branches we should see again, reappearing below, walls, terraces and temples; we should see, stretching away, long paved avenues bordered by so many divinities, seven-headed serpents, bell-turrets, balusters, all in ruins now in the jungle. But the deep forest has again become what it was from the beginning of the ages, during incalculable centuries; there is now no outward sign of the work of those Hindu adventurers, who, some three hundred years before our era, came and plied their axes here, clearing space for a town of nearly a million souls. No; it lasted for but fifteen hundred years, this episode of Khmer empire,[19] that is to say for a very negligible period, in comparison with the longevity of the reign of the vegetable world; and it is finished, the wound is healed, nothing can be seen of it. The fig-tree of the ruins flaunts everywhere its dome of green leaves.

In our days, it is true, some new adventurers, come from a country further to the west (the land of France), are disturbing in a small way the eternal forest, for they have founded not far from here a semblance of a little empire. But this latest episode will lack grandeur, and more especially it will lack duration. Soon, when these pale conquerors will have left in turn, in this Indo-Chinese soil, many of their own—alas, many poor young soldiers not responsible of this mad escapade—they will pack their belongings and flee. Then there will hardly be seen any more wandering in these regions, as I am wandering, men of the white race, who are so foolishly covetous of governing immemorial Asia, and of disturbing everything they find there.

The two fantastic, and almost incandescent keeps, which I was watching from this window, cool with singular rapidity—cool from their base, no doubt because the base is buried in the temple, which in turn is buried in the damp jumble of trees. The red glow persists now only on the topmost point, which suddenly changes to violet and is then extinguished.

The light of the immense panorama dies like the light of a lamp that is blown out, and the forest is already filled with darkness beneath an ash-coloured sky, in which some green and yellow points of light alone indicate the side where the sun has set. The Buddhas around me begin to worry me. I imagine that they are playfully raising their shoulders under the brown layers of droppings which deform them like overlarge fur capes.

The ruins are wrapped in a sudden majesty, so much so that I feel I am profaning the place by being there. And then a

19. The Indianization of Cambodia is predated by Loti by some three hundred years (and Angkor was not its first Indianized centre); the great Angkor period lasted from the ninth to the thirteenth centuries.

nameless horror issues from the darker recesses, where the bent giants, these hunchbacked dwarfs really seem like ghosts. It issues slowly, this insidious horror, trailing along the gallery like a sleepy wave towards the window where I was standing. I realize that it will fill the temple and that I cannot escape it. I must go, therefore, go down in order that I may not be surprised by the darkness in the middle of the staircases, with their slippery steps overgrown with creepers. And, above my head, I can hear the little rat-like cries answering one another along the ceilings of resonant sandstone. It is the hour when all the hairless membranes are about to unfold, to dance in a mad circle around the old sanctuary, to resume the general whirl of every night, the great hunt, the great massacre of gnats and moths.

CHAPTER IX

Saturday, 30th November 1901.

THERE has been another deluge during the night lasting from two o'clock to four, and, although the thatched roof has faithfully protected us, the air is so impregnated with moisture that we awake soaked as by the storm itself.

Now, however, the day is breaking in pure splendour. The blue, cloudless sky remembers nothing of its past. So I have our oxen yoked to our bouncing little carts, in order to return to the forest and visit that temple of the Bayon, of which I had only a glimpse, the day before yesterday, in the rainy twilight.

The sun has not long risen when we leave the wooded enclosure and plunge at the pace of our oxen into the deep forest. At once a green shade stretches over our heads and around us rises the incredible din of birds and insects delirious in their morning joy. Along the pathway, above the impenetrable thickets full of ferns, cycads and orchids, the trees rise to a prodigious height. Amongst them are some that have been scarred by men—even though they are rare and stealthy in these parts—who have notched them in order to collect, in earthen pots, I know not what precious essence. In the same manner one may see, in our country, the inhabitants of the Landes collect the resin of their pines.[1] There are others whose trunks, up to two

1. The Landes is an underpopulated region of sand dunes and pine trees in

metres above the ground, are all scratched, all furrowed with cruel cuts. These are the trees adopted by the tigers, as obsessed in this respect as cats, to stretch their paws and sharpen their claws, when they wake up in the evening after their long daytime siesta.

It is already becoming insufferably hot, with a moist unwholesome heat saturated with exhalations of the lush earth and impetuous plants. In the rays of the sun which, here and there, traverse the foliage, we can see the insects dancing in a circle and their little metallic-lustred bodies throw off sparks of fire. The mosquitoes, those carriers of fever, eddy everywhere in clouds of fine dust. Butterflies, with bodies that are too light for their long silken wings, drift as they fly, as if they were the plaything of the slightest puff of wind, until they settle upon a particular pale-coloured flower of the shade. And the numberless birds which fly before us might be blue or red rockets which we might throw up as we pass through the semi-obscurity of the forest cover.

At the end of nearly an hour the crenellated wall of the mysterious town of Angkor Thom is there before us, without breaking the continuous vault of trees; and still in green night we descend from our ox-carts before the Gate of Victory, above which, beneath a head-dress of creepers, smiles a colossal human visage.

About half an hour's walk, in this forest strewn with debris, which is the winding sheet of a town, where every stone bears trace of an antique carving, where the fragments one picks up in the grass represent a human mask. And then we reach a shapeless mass of rocks, a kind of mountain above which those fig-trees of the ruins proudly spread their large green parasols. Here it is. These rocks were built long ago by the hand of man; they are artificial; they are the remains of one of the most prodigious temples of the world.

---

southwest France. The Cambodians were collecting tree sap, used, inter alia, for lighting torches.

The destruction is bewildering. How could these masses of stone have been thrown down in this way, to lean, to crumble, to merge into chaos? There are towers which seem to have slipped down as one piece, to have descended in their entirety from their foundations. The massive terraces have given way. And all around the earth has risen; the humus, in the course of centuries, has begun to climb the broad staircases in its attempt to swallow everything.

The immense faces of Brahma,[2] "the gracious old ladies," so sly-looking and so little reassuring the other evening in the twilight, I see them again everywhere above my head, smiling upon me from between the ferns and roots. They are far more numerous than I thought. I can discern them even on the most distant of the towers, crowned and with necklaces around their necks. But in broad daylight, how they have lost their power to scare one! They seem to say to me this morning: "We are quite dead, you see, and quite harmless. It is not out of irony we smile thus, with eyelids half-closed; it is because we have now attained peace without dreams."

The temple, the scarcely recognizable ruins of which are in front of me, represents the impulsive conception, artless and powerfully savage, of a people apart, without counterpart in the world, and without neighbours: the Khmer people, a detached branch of the great Aryan race, which planted itself here by chance, and developed far from its original source, separated from the rest of the world by immense expanses of forest and marshland. About the ninth century, some four hundred years earlier than Angkor Wat,[3] this sanctuary, cruder and more enormous, was in all its glory. In order to try and picture what was once its awe-inspiring magnificence, it would be necessary, first of all, to clear away, in imagination, its forest, to suppress

2. They were not Brahman in their final form, but represented the bodhisattva Avolekitesvara.

3. The Bayon and Angkor Thom were built by Jayavarman VII in the late twelfth—early thirteenth centuries, some fifty years after the construction of Angkor Wat.

the inextricable entanglement of these roots and these greenish white-spotted branches, which are, as it were, the tentacles of the fig-tree of the ruins; and then, no longer in this eternal green night, but in the open air, under the wide sky, to re-erect these towers with four faces—about fifty towers![4]—to replace them upright on their monstrous pedestal, which like that at Angkor Wat had three levels. To imagine, next, all around, an expanse of empty space, so that men might see from afar the crushing stature of the whole; to reconstruct the successive terraces, the steps, the sumptuous avenues which led here, bordered by so many columns, balusters, divinities, and monsters, which today lie collapsed in the grass.

These towers with their squat forms and superposed rows of crowns might be compared in outline to colossal pine cones placed upright. It was as if a vegetation of stone had sprouted in thick impetuous profusion from the soil; fifty towers of different heights rising in tiers; fifty fantastic pine cones grouped in bundles on a base as large as a town, almost linked to one another and forming a procession to a central and more gigantic tower, sixty or seventy metres in height, which dominated them, its summit crowned with a golden lotus-flower. And from high in the air, those four faces which each bore gazed at the four cardinal points, gazed everywhere, with the same lowered eyelids, the same expression of ironical pity, the same smile. They affirmed, they repeated obsessively, the omnipresence of the god of Angkor. From the different points of the immense town these aerial faces were always to be seen, some full-face, others in profile or three-quarter face, now gloomy under lowering rain-charged skies, now ardent, as with ruddy fire, at the setting of the torrid sun, or again, bluish and ghostly on moonlit nights, but always there and always commanding. But today their reign is over; in the green half-light in which they are disintegrating it is necessary, almost, to seek to find them, and the time is approaching when they will no longer even be recognizable.

4. Fifty-four, as indicated in note 11 on page 38.

To ornament the walls of the Bayon, endless bas-reliefs and decorative scrolls of every sort have been conceived with an exuberant prodigality. Here, too, there are battles, furious conflicts, war chariots, interminable processions of elephants, and groups of Apsaras, of Tevadas[5] with pompous crowns. But under the moss everything is becoming effaced and perishing. The workmanship is cruder and more childish than at Angkor Wat, but the inspiration revealed here is more violent, more tumultuous. There is something disconcerting in so great a profusion. In our days of versatile shabbiness it is difficult to realize the perseverance, the wealth, the faith, the love of the grand and the eternal, which inspired this vanished people.

Beneath the central tower with its golden lotus, some twenty metres above the plain, the Holy of Holies is hidden, a dark retreat, stifling as a casemate in the thickness of the stone. It was approached from many sides, by a complex of converging galleries, as mournful as sepulchral chambers. But access to it today is difficult and dangerous; the approaches have so many rockfalls. You feel that you are still beneath the forest—for the forest covers even the towers—beneath a multiple and uncountable network of innumerable roots. It is almost dark. A lukewarm water oozes from all the walls, over some phantom gods without arms or without a head. You can hear the gliding of snakes, the flight of indeterminate crawling beasts; and the bats awake, flicking you, by way of protest, with their rapidly moving membranes which you had not seen coming. In Brahmanistic times this Holy of Holies[6] must have been a place where men trembled, and centuries of neglect have not robbed it of its awe. It still remains the refuge of the ancient mysteries. The noises made by the furtive beasts as we entered cease as soon as we become still, and everything subsides at once into an intense silence, filled with I know not what horror of expectancy.

5. Thevada, sometimes devata, from Sanskrit *deva*, the celestial inhabitants of one of the lower heavens of the Buddhist cosmology.

6. As implied in note 11 on page 38, the Bayon was not in its final form a Brahmanical monument, but Buddhist.

In this forest of shadow are to be found a number of other ruins, in disjointed and overthrown masses, beneath the beautiful, triumphant branches; debris of palaces, of temples, of bathing places where men and elephants used to wash. They still bear witness to the splendour of that empire of the Khmers, which flourished for fifteen hundred years unknown to Europe, and then perished after a swift decline, exhausted by a succession of wars with Siam, with Annam, and even with immemorial and stagnant China.[7]

To my western eyes, I come away with an overriding impression of bafflement and mystery from these dead things. The least carving, the least lintel over a portico, the least of these crowns imitating flames, is a cause of astonishment, like the revelation of a distant and hostile world. Monsters in greenish stone, seated like dogs, and with their heads probably adorned in the fashion of some planet not in communication with ours, welcome me with looks of excessive strangeness, with a rictus never previously seen, not even in the old Chinese sanctuaries from which I have come. "We do not know you," they say to me. "We are conceptions forever foreign to you. What are you doing here? Be off with you!" Moreover, as the sun rises and blazes more fiercely above the thick vault of the trees, an increasing heaviness slows down our steps; as we walk we are more and more closely enveloped by a kind of aggressive dust, dancing and sparkling, which is a cloud of mosquitoes; and it is with a rather feverish lassitude that we continue to wander in this forest of dark enchantments. Enough! It is time to retrace our steps towards the Gate of Victory, in order to return before midday to the enclosure of Angkor Wat.

The burning hour is near when we are again sheltered by the pilgrims' shed, where is heard from morning till evening, like an incantation, the psalmody of the yellow-robed monks.

And, after the midday meal, the irresistible tropical languor

7. Poetic licence: ancient Cambodia was never at war with China, nor indeed with Vietnam, though its conflicts with Champa, and later with nascent Siam, were almost continuous.

returns, as it returns every day, to make us torpid. It would be better to leave this shed in which one stifles, and, braving the biting sun, cross the ten metres or so which separate me from the first galleries of the temple. In the shadow and perpetual dampness of the stone ceilings I may find at least an appearance of coolness. Let someone spread a mat there for me, after sweeping clear a space at a point where the vault is not too festooned with bats, and I shall sleep on the comparatively cool flagstones, covering my face with a fan as a protection from what may fall from the roof.

However, sleep is slow in coming to me, for I am lying at the very foot of the immense bas-relief of battles, and, spite of me, my heavy eyes are intrigued by it for a long time: silent torment; fury of great conflicts past and forgotten, slaughters sung by the poets of the Ramayana, but which no one any more remembers; confusion of muscular arms and calves meeting in shock of battle between the army of the Giants and that of the King of the Monkeys,[8] war chariots crushing the wounded in hundreds. In the prevailing gloom, all this, blackish and, as if varnished by the damp, is brightened in places by a glimmering half-light, and thus the reliefs are accentuated, a little life returns to the effaced rictus, to the dead contortions. I have lost the notion of the enormity of the mass of architecture all around, but I feel that I have become intimate with those of the warriors, men and women, who struggle near me, almost touching my head. Quite near an Apsara smiles upon me in the confusion. Hers is the last image I am conscious of. For some minutes more I see her fair breast gleaming, looking moist as if it were beaded with a warm perspiration and then, no more; I lapse into unconsciousness.

I have perhaps been asleep for an hour, when one of my Siamese servants brings me the cards of three visitors. The names are French. Yes, by all means show them in here, into my splendid reception hall. But truly, it is the last thing I should have expected: to receive visitors at Angkor.

8. Hanuman.

Three Frenchmen in fact. They have been sent to Siam for archaeological studies, and since yesterday have been installed, not far from me, beneath a roof of thatch in the holy enclosure.* They are erudite and pleasant. Besides, after days of solitude and silence, travelling without companions, it is relaxing to exchange thoughts with men from France.

I ought to remain, they tell me, for the forest is full of unknown ruins. In addition to the great temples which everyone sees, there are to be found scattered about, by the side of the rivers and swamps, a number of monuments in terracotta of a most unusual design, dating back to the fourth century, or to the earliest days of the vast Khmer empire.

But no; I will adhere to my intention of leaving today when the sun goes down. First, there are the elephants of the good King Norodom which I am due to meet the day after tomorrow at Kampong Luong. And then, and more especially, how should I forget that I am, in fact, no more than a modest aide-de-camp, whose leave is limited, and must return within the stipulated time, on board the battleship which awaits me at Saigon?

I have given the order to prepare our departure for five o'clock; and, while the ox-carts are being got ready and my kit is being packed, I mount the steps of the temple for the last time.

No rain has fallen since last night to water the hanging plants, or moisten the heaps of stones, and an intolerable heat, as of glowing embers, now emanates from the terraces, the walls and carvings on which the sun has been blazing all day long. But the divine Apsaras, who have been used for centuries to be burnt in this way by the sun's rays, smile goodbye to me, without losing their ease or customary gracious irony. As I took leave of them I

*** One of them, son of a famous French sculptor, was not long in dying afterwards of forest fever.**[9]

9. This was Charles Carpeaux, son of the well-known sculptor Jean- Baptiste Carpeaux, who was sent to Angkor by the EFEO with the architect Henri Dufour, to prepare a book about the Bayon, which was published in Paris in 1910. Charles Carpeaux died in Saigon in 1904, aged thirty-three. In his notebooks, published in 1908, he mentions meeting Loti.

little thought that within a few hours, by the lavish caprice of the King of Phnom Penh, I should see them again, one night, accompanied by the evocative sound of the ancient music of their times, see them no longer dead, with these fixed smiles of stone, but in the fulness of life and youth, no longer with these breasts of rigid sandstone, but with palpitating breasts of flesh, and wearing veritable tiaras of gold, and sparkling with veritable jewels.

The sun is already low and beginning to give out a reddish light when my little procession of ox-carts gets under way, leaving Angkor behind forever, along the paved causeway, between the bushes clustered with the white flowers of fragrant jasmine. Beyond the broad moats full of reeds and lotus, beyond the bridge, the last porticoes and the great seven-headed serpents which guard the threshold, here is the path of departure before us. It plunges under the trees which are ready at once to hide the mysterious temple from us. I turn, therefore, to take a last look at Angkor. This pilgrimage, which since my childhood I had hoped to make, is now a thing accomplished, and has fallen into the past, as one day will fall my own brief human existence, and I shall never see again, rising into the sky, those great strange towers. I cannot even, this last time, follow them for long with my eyes, for immediately the forest closes round us, suddenly ushering in the twilight.

At about seven or eight o'clock we reach the Siamese village of Siem Reap, on the bank of the river, in the region of tall palms. It is quite dark, and the half-naked people who move about under the vault of trees get the light they need by waving burning brands, as is the custom also in India on the Malabar coast.[10] They hasten to welcome us and install us, on the river bank, in a hut used by travelling pilgrims, which seems to be on stilts, so high are the piles on which it is raised.

10. Loti described this in more detail in *Mahé des Indes*; he had visited the French colony, a dependency of Pondichéry on the southeast coast of India, in 1884 when his ship stopped briefly in Colombo.

CHAPTER X

Sunday, 1st December 1901.

AN hour more in our ox-carts, along the bank of the little river, in the freshness of the early morning, passing through Eden-like villages, amongst palms and garlands of flowering creepers.

At a point on the bank the sampan which brought us here was waiting for us—the large sampan, with a roof shaped like a coffin lid. Then, leaving our carts, we begin to go down the river, brushed by reeds, and by giant grasses. First of all, swamps ever more flooded, and then the submerged forest, which, as it envelops us in its poisonous shadow, takes away the little air there was to breathe. An hour and a half of rowing, to cross the almost gloomy labyrinth, passing between enormous half-submerged trees, amongst branches entangled with creepers. It is only about midday that we escape from the oppression of the forest and that the great lake, opening at last ahead of us, spreads before our eyes, which are suddenly dazzled at the expanse of a sea of gleaming tin.

The steamboat which is to take us back to Cambodia is there, alone, moored to the branches of this semblance of a shore, looking as if it were lost in the midst of this desert of verdure and warm water. Let us get up steam and leave as soon as possible.

All the afternoon, all the evening, is spent in gliding, with rapid and monotonous motion, over this lake which today has no visible limits, to such a degree does the mist it gives off blur the horizon. The sun seems to vaporize it, to drink it—a sun that, all imbued with moisture as well, seems almost troubled, as well as shifty and terrible. Not a breath of wind anywhere, and enough electric tension to kill one. Our steamboat makes always the same little ridges on the mournful water, which silently reproduce themselves and disappear. We seem to be sailing on some molten metal, too listless or too heavy to make a noise like ordinary water, and in this way we rock to sleep the flocks of pelicans we pass, stretched out in long bands of pinkish-white, scarcely disturbed by our approach. Everywhere, somnolence and torpor under a light at once excessive and diffuse. From time to time there are enacted before us phantasmagorias to scare us: they appear, always, in the west. We see sombre objects rising in the distance, almost as quickly as the smoke from volcanoes. They darken a whole side of the sky; they take on shades of copper; they assume the appearance of toppling rocks, of mountains about to tumble into chaos: rough shapings of storms which do not break, but are transformed at once, dissolving and vanishing like the visions of dreams.

Not a boat in sight, not a junk: we are alone upon this shoreless sea. Through all these insubstantialities of sky and water, without any kind of landmark, our pilot—a Siamese—guides himself by instinct, no doubt, in the same way as migrating birds. In the twilight, however, when he needs to find the entrance to the great river down which we must proceed, he is perplexed, he hesitates and changes route. There is no danger, however, only the risk of being detained here until daybreak.

CHAPTER XI

Monday, 2nd December 1901.

AT about three o'clock this morning, under a deluge in which all the clouds of yesterday were emptying themselves, we had come to a mooring amongst the reeds of the great river, near the village of Kampong Luong. It is here that the river brings me closest to a certain temple dedicated to the spirit of the queen mother of Cambodia, to which I intend, in passing, to make a pilgrimage. It lies some distance away in the dense undergrowth.

Now, at daybreak, I am awakened by formidable footsteps, which make the adjacent bank tremble, and are accompanied by a music of snapping branches. Through a porthole, open near my head, I look to see what ponderous visitors have come. The just dawning day reveals a jumble of reeds and damp bushes, which already seem too vividly green for so dim a light, just as the earth, too, seems already too red. And in this setting of the early morning colossal beasts appear, gambolling in clumsy playfulness, and shaking the earth. It might be some scene from the morning of the world. Elephants! Without doubt the four promised elephants, and they have come punctually to the rendezvous. Four men, dressed in white, follow them, talking gently to them, and at an order given almost in a whisper, they become motionless just in front of me.

When the good elephants are saddled, having each on its nape a squatting driver, and on its back a palanquin like a Cambodian hut, I am invited to take my place, with my interpreter and my two servants. We set off one behind the other, each of us in his little oscillating lodge. We have to go, first of all, through the village. Then the market, where a small crowd of yellow people has come from the nearby undergrowth on foot or by cart, to buy and sell fruit, grain, chickens, and strange fish from the Mekong. Our elephants, aware of the fear they are about to cause, only walk here with short, quiet steps, but, as invariably happens, all the oxen, all the buffaloes flee before the sovereign beast, and some wicker crates are knocked over, some bowls of milk upset—there is tumult and cries.

After this isolated grouping of human life, we plunge for two or three hours into the dense undergrowth and meet not a soul on our way. There is no forest of shadows here as in Siam, but simply undergrowth, that Indo-Chinese undergrowth, inextricable, always the same, useless and endless. We follow narrow pathways, on a red soil of bloodstone, between two curtains of bushes of excessively brilliant green. Foliage which is strange to us imprisons us more and more in its multitudinous compactness: a whole vegetation eternally watered, eternally overheated, which even so does not succeed in producing mature trees, but remains stunted, soft and of an unhealthy exuberance. From the vantage of our palanquins we see from time to time unlimited expanses of this sad verdure, which tells of exile and savours of fever.

In the foreground, in front of me, always the bronze neck of the mahout, and now and then, two enormous grey ears which rise and beat the air like fans. One has a sense of princely well-being in the little rocking lodge, sheltered from the fiery sun, travelling in this sure and solid fashion, with a step that never stumbles, and a calm that no obstacle will have the strength to disturb. And yet in time the heart begins to sicken a little at the monotony of this undergrowth which closes behind you in silence, ceaselessly, mercilessly, as the minutes pass.

We make our midday halt at an old monastery at the foot of a little mountain, which serves as a pedestal to the mausoleum of the Cambodian kings. Here there is some running water and trees that are really tall; this is a little corner of paradise in the midst of this desert of unhealthy verdure. A vast hall of reddish wood, with a distorted roof, having by way of walls little more than reed blinds, and decorated with huge Buddhist pictures on rice paper, which are hung from the pillars. We install ourselves there on mats, welcomed with fitting dignity by two or three aged monks, and a grandmother of a nun with white close-cropped hair, whose face of parchment bears the impress of a hundred years. Our elephants have been let loose in the undergrowth where they will eat for their dinner a few young trees. Treading on tiptoe, the venerable old lady in her religious garb of yellow[1] brings us square-shaped pillows on which to lean or lay our head. She says nothing, and her features, transfixed by so many years of a mysticism unintelligible to our souls, do not move. After the midday meal we fall asleep, stretched out on our mats, in a very special kind of monastic peace, listening to the sound of the nearby stream, which gives an illusion of coolness.

About half-past three comes the awakening, for my attendants as well as for myself, and I order the elephants to be brought back, for it is time to resume our journey.

This mountain which overhangs the monastery is one of those geological fantasies which are scattered here and there in the midst of the low-lying plains of Cambodia: one of those abrupt, isolated, unexpected cones which are known here as *pnom.* They are nearly all holy, and serve as a base to a place of prayer. This particular one, already very pointed in itself, is made more so by the mausoleum which caps it and is more pointed, more slender than any of our cathedral spires. And it is there, high above the jungle full of tigers and monkeys, which surrounds it, as near as possible to the stormy sky, that the old kings of Cambodia sleep.

1. Loti's memory is at fault: only Buddhist monks wear yellow, nuns wear white.

The ashes of the queen mother have been deposited there recently after a cremation which observed immemorial rites, with a ceremonial of dance and music dating back without any doubt to the Angkorean period.

It is about an hour's journey from the monastery to the shrine consecrated to the spirit of this old princess, which is the goal of my pilgrimage. The sun is getting low when we see it, in a kind of clearing in the middle of the undergrowth. Amongst tall, slender palm trees, the green fronds of which dominate the surrounding jungle, it appears before us all illuminated by the Bengal lights of the setting sun, its tarnished gildings gleaming softly like some precious piece of antique goldsmith's craft. Its image is reflected in a solitary pool strewn with islets of pink lotus. It is ornamented, needless to say, with long, golden finials, which stand out from the roof at every angle, and it is raised on a triple-stepped base, on the edges of which monsters, in attitudes of mockery, are consumed with laughter, with the frightening laughter of a death's head. Hearing our elephants approaching, some of the monks, robed in lemon-yellow and draped in orange-yellow, open the doors and stand in groups at different levels on the steps of the threshold. It is a perfect vision of the old ages of Asia that was awaiting us in the silence of this remote spot and in the red glow of evening.

I am advised by my interpreter that it would be more discreet on my part, and more *gracious*, not to ask the monks, who would not dare refuse me, for permission to visit the interior of the shrine. Without coming down from my palanquin, I confine myself, therefore, to going slowly around it.

It is the art of Angkor that one finds again here, greatly reduced, of course, from its colossal proportions, and a little too affected, perhaps, too mannered, but still of a most exquisite strangeness. At Angkor the enormous walls were covered with embroideries of stone. Here, beneath the fantastic roof with its great golden finials, the whole shrine seems to be hung with a sumptuous old brocade, which scintillates in the dying rays of the sun—it is a veritable network of minute carvings in gilded stucco, in which are mingled particles of glass imitating rubies and emeralds. And the doors, which shine with a different and bluish lustre, are in a mosaic of mother-of-pearl.

Our elephants, as if they realized that we wished to view the shrine without haste, make the circuit of the terraces with a somnolent majesty. One after another, each of the statues, placed at the edges, presents to us, as we pass, its ironic grimace. They have the bodies of men, but the faces of scarecrows; they represent the guardian spirits of the eternal thresholds; and their presence suffices to mark a burial place and to command reflection. All with legs apart and hands resting on their bent knees, they look as if they stooped the better to laugh at human frailty, no doubt, laughing at birth and at death. As on the walls of the shrine, the guardian monsters are covered with gilded carvings and facets of glass, which give them costumes of great pomp, a little faded with time, it is true, and spotted with grey mould. As for their faces, they are already familiar to us; they have been copied from the thousand-year-old bas-reliefs of Angkor Wat. But why these convulsed attitudes of macabre laughter in this place of supreme peace? To us what an abyss of mystery there is in this conception of tombs!

When we have completed the circuit of the shrine, and return once more before the mother-of-pearl doors, it is only the gold of the roof, its somewhat Chinese curves and its long finials which shine brilliantly. The sun has finished drowning itself in the endless verdure of the plains. It no longer illumines the walls, and we see these old brocades, already faded by the rains of many seasons, dimmed with subtle shadings, and where in only a few places gleams a kind of glass embroidery. The monks, to do us honour, have remained standing on the steps. And all that—the shrine, these motionless people in yellow robes, the funereal spirits laughing at the edges of the terraces, with hands resting on their outspread knees—is reflected in the dead waters of the pond, where the lotus, flowers of broad daylight, are beginning to draw together and close their wide pink petals because the shadows of evening are falling. Upon these antiquated splendours there seems to descend more and more, as the twilight deepens, the peace of profound isolation.

It is time to go, and the pace of our elephants quickens for the return journey. We plunge again into the narrow pathways, where we are hemmed in and brushed continually by the verdure. Once more the undergrowth closes in behind us, the eternal undergrowth, hastening to hide from us the magic clearing, which, perhaps, is still occasionally haunted by the incomprehensible soul of an old queen of the Far East.

It is completely dark when the good giant beasts kneel down to deposit us at the village of this morning, near the bank of the river. The boat, already under steam, is awaiting us there. I order the anchor to be weighed and continue the journey down the Mekong. It is the time of the year when the waters of the lakes of Siam are emptied into the great river, and we set out with all the speed of our engines aided by the swiftness of the current. A little after midnight we reach Phnom Penh again, the almost French colonial town, and are moored before the gardens of the governor.

CHAPTER XII

Tuesday, 3rd December 1901.

AT Phnom Penh until the following midnight, after which it will be necessary to withdraw to Saigon, so as to be on board at the expiration of my leave. A warm, torrential rain the whole day long.

This evening at nine o'clock old King Norodom is to receive me. And as the governor had the great kindness to intimate to him that I was not an ordinary aide-de-camp, but a French man of letters, it appears that there is to be a grand reception in which the royal *corps de ballet* will figure.

The rain is still falling in a deluge when the governor's carriage comes to take me to the palace. The night is suffocating, in spite of the tropical downpour which descends upon us from the black sky. Our way lies under jumbled trees, along dark avenues where nothing seems to be alive. But a blaze of light greets us on arrival, and attendants, carring broad Asiatic umbrellas, hurry forward to assist us in alighting, and to shelter us in our passage to the reception hall.

It is immense, this hall, but it has no walls, nothing but a roof upheld in the air by very tall blue pillars. In the girandoles and on the Cambodian silver candelabra—where not long ago burnt only wicks soaked in oil—electric light has recently been installed. It is little disconcerting here, and brutally splashes the crowd of princesses, ladies-in-waiting, attendants, musicians, some five or six hundred people in all, seated on mats on the floor. All the costumes are white as are all the draperies, and there is a multitude of bare arms and bare bosoms the colour of pale bronze. The orchestra, as soon as we appear, begins, an Asiatic music which straightaway transports us into far distances of space and time. It is slow and powerful, rendered by some thirty instruments of metal or resonant wood, which are struck with velvet-topped drumsticks. There are dulcimers, wooden xylophones with a very extended keyboard, and peals of little gongs which vibrate in the manner of pianos played with the loud pedal. The melody is infinitely sad, but the rhythm increases feverishly as with a tarantella.

We are seated on a platform near the golden-mattressed couch on which presently the old, infirm, and almost dying king will come to lie. Near us, on an elegent gilt table, are tall champange glasses, and boxes, made of the reddish Cambodian gold, filled with cigarettes. We dominate the hall, the centre of which, carpeted with white mats and large enough for manoeuvring a battalion, is empty. It is there that the ballet performance will take place for us. Over-large vases, filled with foliage as subtle as flowers, are placed at the foot of each of the blue pillars. Between the pillars, above the white-clothed crowd, can be seen the black of the rainy night, the profound darkness of the sky; at present, one can see above all the rain, which is now coming down in torrents more furious than ever. The smallest drops, in passing into the vivid electric light, throw off prismatic sparks, and shine so that one seems to see precious stones falling by the thousand, and diamonds in cascades. Two doors at the further end open into the interior of the palace, and it is from these that the ballerinas will appear. The heat remains overpowering, in spite of the broad fans which are waved unceasingly above our heads by the attendants. And everywhere innumerable flights of insects, maddened by the brilliance of the girandoles, whirl; mosquitoes, mayflies, humming beetles, and large moths.

The king is long in coming, and now attendants bring his gold crown and sceptre, set with large rubies and emeralds, and place them on a cushion near us. He is after all too ill;* he requests that we will excuse him, and sends us these attributes of sovereignty to intimate to us that the reception is, nevertheless, a royal one.

The performance, then, will begin without him. The music suddenly becomes quieter and more mysterious, as if it were announcing something supernatural. One of the doors at the back opens; an adorable and almost visionary little creature springs into the middle of the hall—an Apsara from the temple at Angkor! It would be impossible to imagine a more perfect illusion. She has the same features because she is of the same pure race, the same enigmatic smile, the eyes downcast, almost closed, the same very young virgin's breasts scarcely veiled by a thin silk net. And her costume is scrupulously copied from the old bas-reliefs, but copied in real jewels, in gorgeous fabrics; kinds of sheaths of gold brocade imprison her legs and loins. Her face whitened with make-up, her eyes artificially elongated, she wears a very high golden tiara studded with rubies, which tapers to a point like the roof of a temple, and on either shoulder a kind of wing-tip, like a dolphin's fin, in gold and precious stones. Of gold likewise, set with precious stones, are the broad waistband, the rings which ornament her ankles and her bare arms the colour of slightly pink amber. At first alone on the stage, this little Apsara of remote ages, having escaped from the sacred bas-relief, makes signs of calling to someone in the direction of the door in the background—which has become for us the door of

*** He died a short time afterwards. And it is his successor, King Sisovath, who visited France, and committed the amiable fault of showing to the Parisians some of his court ballerinas. One ought not to profane and diminish such performances by presenting them in this way devoid of their setting.**[1]

1. King Norodom, aged sixty-six in 1901, was to die three years later. Sisowath (1840–1927) succeeded him in 1904, and visited France for a month in 1906; his daughter went along as supervisor of the *corps de ballet* which accompanied his visit. At a garden party at the Elysée Palace on 1 July, a performance (adjudged highly erotic by blasé Parisians) was given by the ballerinas. Another was given in Marseilles at the Colonial Exhibition.

fairy-like apparitions—and two of her sisters run out to join her, two new Apsaras, likewise sparkling, their hips moulded in the same rigid sheaths, wearing the same golden crowns and the same golden wing-tips. All three join hands. They are, doubtless, the queens of the Apsaras, for thrones have been prepared for them to sit on. But they mime anxiety, and begin again to make signs of calling, always in the direction of that same door. We have already marvelled at seeing three. Can it be that there are others still to come? And now they appear in groups, ten, twenty, thirty, bedecked like goddesses as were the first, wearing on their charming heads and shoulders all the riches of Cambodia.

Before the three seated queens, they proceed to perform their ritual dances, which involve little or no change of place, but consist rather in rhythmic quiverings of the whole body. They undulate like snakes, these slender little creatures, their exquisitely muscular bodies which seem to have no bones. At times they spread out their arms in the form of a cross, and then the serpentine undulation begins in the fingers of the right hand, flows through the wrist, the forearm, the elbow, the shoulder, crosses the breast, and continues on the opposite side, following the other arm until it dies at last on the tips of the fingers of the left hand, overloaded with rings.

In real life these exquisite little ballerinas are very jealously guarded children, often indeed princesses of the royal blood, whom no one has the right either to approach or see. They have been trained from their earliest years to perform these movements which do not seem possible for human limbs; to produce these poses which are so unnatural, but are, nevertheless, of immemorial tradition in this country, as is proved by the stone inhabitants of the ruins.

They are going to mime now some scenes from the Ramayana, such as formerly were carved in hard sandstone, in the bas-reliefs of the ancestral temple. The handsome war chariots, copied in miniature from those of Angkor Wat, make their entry. But, by a naive convention, the elephants which should be drawing them have been replaced by men, walking on all fours, naked and yellow, masked in huge cardboard heads with moveable trunks and ears. Then we watch different gracious or tragic episodes, combats with monsters, above all march pasts and processions to celebrate victories. We see a little queen of fourteen or fifteen years, very much bejewelled, very much made-up, immaculate in her war chariot, pursued by the declarations of love of a young warrior, and repulsing them with infinitely chaste grace. We see a thousand delicate and charming things which testify to an art of the most refined kind. Whenever a procession of Apsaras withdraws by one of the doors in the rear, another procession enters from the other door and proceeds slowly to occupy the hall. There are some of these little fairies, all in gold, who can be no more than seven or eight years old; and they file past, painted like images, crowned with over-high tiaras, with jewelled wing-tips on their shoulders, grave and dignified in their sacerdotal attitudes.

An ever more oppressive heat is exhaled from this crowd, which is perfumed with musk and flowers; the torrential rain continues to fill the background of the scene with its stream of sparkling gems; from all the neighbouring undergrowth, myriads of little winged insects come to hurl themselves endlessly against the lamps and candelabra; large bats and nocturnal birds also appear; the exuberant animal life, with which the air is filled to excess, envelops and penetrates us.

Now comes the 'King of the Monkeys' grimacing, in his mask of gold, just as I have seen him, needless to say, carved on the walls of the old temples. He also assumes poses which are not natural, are not possible (always the poses of the bas-reliefs); his youthful limbs have been adapted from very early days to these exigencies of tradition. In his train the whole army of monkeys invades the scene: young girls again, little princesses masked like scarecrows, but whose filling breasts are outlined underneath light and costly silks. And the object is for this astonishing but scarcely dangerous cohort to go to the rescue of fair Sita, whom the demons hold captive, a very long way off, on an island. We are in the midst of the Ramayana, and the same performances were once enacted, no doubt, at Angkor Thom, the same costumes were worn there. This evening we are able to imagine, better than ever before, what were the splendours of the legendary town. Epochs we thought were gone forever come to life again before our eyes. But it is not a careful recreation which revives them. No, quite simply nothing has changed here, whether in the souls of men or in the secrets of palaces, since heroic times. In spite of its diminished outward appearances, this fallen Cambodian race has remained the Khmer people, the people which astonished the Asia of olden times by its pomp and mysticism. One knows, too, that it has never surrendered its hope of reconquering its great capital, buried for centuries now in the forests of Siam; and it is always the Ramayana, that epic so ancient and so nebulous, which continues to haunt its imagination and to direct its dream.

Let us hope that France, the protectress (?) of this land, may be able to understand that the ballet of the kings of Phnom Penh is a sacred heritage, a marvel of antiquity not to be destroyed!

At about one o'clock in the morning, in the dark night and under the warm rain, we leave Norodom's palace, and I go to have the steamboat, which awaits me, made ready for departure. I start to go down the Mekong again in deep and oppressive darkness, and for me the vision of the little fairies of the Ramayana vanishes.

The day after tomorrow I must be back in Saigon, that graceless town of languor and death, to take my place again in attendance on the admiral, amongst my companions in exile; to shut myself up once more within the stifling iron walls of that battleship, which, for nearly twenty-two months, has carried us through all the swells of the seas of China, but which sleeps now alongside a morbid quay, where the verdure of the trees is too vividly green, and the soil sadly reddish.

CHAPTER XIII

October 1910.

NEARLY ten more years have passed since my pilgrimage. And now the hour has come, quickly, stealthily, the hour which it seemed to me should never come, the twilight hour of life when all earthly things grow distant, diminish, and are blurred with grey shadows.

After a luminous summer, perhaps the last, spent in the East,[1] I returned this morning to my parental home. This corner of France on which my eyes opened is fine today, calm under a blue sky; but the sun, which is still clear and warm, has a touch of pallor, which marks the end of the season and adds to the melancholy of my return.

And here now chance has brought me back to this little retreat which was the museum of my childhood—a little room whose door I hardly ever think of opening, but which I allowed to continue to exist as a place for souvenirs.

The poor things, which once so filled my mind with thoughts of distant countries, are withering and crumbling in their little glass cases, like mummies abandoned in their chamber. There is a faded odour of camphor, of stuffed birds, an indefinable air of mortality, and it is sad here, this evening, unspeakably so. I open

1. Loti had just returned from Constantinople, where he had been from 15 August to 23 October 1910. It was his sixth journey to Turkey, and not his last—he went again for a month in 1913.

the window. But it seems to me that everything becomes more mournful still when I let in the rays of the sun of this October evening. Ah, a wasp has entered at the same time. I remember how formerly many wasps used to come in here, for the little room opens onto the gardens, onto old narrow provincial gardens, the walls of which are covered with vines and rose-trees.

I think of it suddenly, that out-of-date copy of a colonial review containing the pictures which were the first to reveal to me the ruins of Angkor. It should still be there, behind a curtain. How is it that it did not occur to me to look for it on my return from the Far East? I shall try to find it now in this recess, where the dust lies thick like impalpable ash.

It was certainly decisive, the influence this museum exercised in the orientation of my life. This is true for most men, simple playthings as they are of their first impressions; trifles for long observed in childhood suffice, one way or another, to change the direction of all their subsequent destiny. And this evening—is it because I have not seen it for so many months, my tiny museum?—its spell might almost still work. The poor objects on its shelves almost induce in me the restlessness and the thrill of unknown countries, to which to run and escape. How childish the feeling is! It is finished, all that; the unknown exists no longer, and I have drained the cup of adventures to the dregs. The brilliant bird behind this glass case once made me dream of the "colonies," but I have visited the most impenetrable of the forests in which it dwelt. That humble calabash, with its primitive designs, I used to think of as a precious curiosity, but I have lived amongst the black Yoloffs [2] who excel in carving them like this, in the shadow of their reed roofs, before their sandy horizons. That paddle, hanging on the wall, once conjured up visions of savage islanders, but the Polynesians have taught me how to handle similar ones, together with them, in canoes rocked in the swell of the great ocean. Is that, then, all the world is? Is life no more than that?

2. Wolofs, in Senegal, whom Loti got to know in 1873–1874.

Ah! I have found the copy of the colonial review containing the revelation of Angkor. How imperfect and clumsy the pictures seem on this yellowing paper, compared with the admirable illustrations we are used to today! Alas, they date back some half-century. They are very faithful, nevertheless, and show clearly the tall turrets, in outline like tiaras, which I have since seen in reality, under the tropical sun and under lowering storm clouds. As soon as I have seen these unpretentious drawings, immediately, of course, the impressions when seeing them the first time crowd back into my memory. Even those emphatic phrases of Ecclesiastes, which then rang through in my childish head, come back as if they were from yesterday: "I have tried all things, I have experienced everything... In the depths of the forests of Siam, I have seen the evening star rise over the ruins of mysterious Angkor."

But today is the day of that mournful return home of which I had so clear a presentiment, the last return of all, with heavy heart and greying hair. The fact cannot be ignored; it is today, the cycle of my life is closed.

Some wasps still come in, and so do buzzing flies; before the little sealed glass showcases and the little dead things, they trace their foolish curves. The time is near, however, when they will go to sleep or die; but no doubt because of tradition, they light-heartedly reappear in this place which has been closed for so long, where they used formerly to dance giddily in my company. The smallest insects, everyone knows, repeat eternally the same things in the same places, just as the tiny mosses and small wild flowers come to life again for centuries in the same corner of the woods.

To turn over the pages of this ancient, out-of-date review, I have sat down near the open window. The late October sun is sinking over the plain of Aunis[3] which I can see beyond the neighbouring roofs and the ramparts. On the far horizon there

3. See note 8 on page 12. A small former coastal province in western France, with its old centre in La Rochelle.

are still the same woods, adjoining those of Limoise,[4] and their contours have not changed. In the distance, amidst the meadows, the Charente[5] traces its thin, shining trail, and formerly this river by which the ships made their way to exotic countries, to the "colonies," represented for me the gateway into the unknown; but where would it lead me now, to what oceans that I have not explored? In the review resting on my knee, I discover pictures which I had not noticed or had forgotten: here is the great mask of Brahma with its mocking expression such as it appeared to me one evening in the forest of shadow, multiplied in a frightening way and gazing down upon me from the top of the towers with four faces. I did not suspect that it had been lying in wait for me so many years, on a dusty shelf, amongst the personal knick-knacks of my childhood. On the next page are three Apsaras from the bas-reliefs, with rounded bosoms copied from models which throbbed a thousand years before. They take me back in my mind to the ballet of the kings of Phnom Penh, which was like the apotheosis of my pilgrimage, a veritable blaze of gold, colour and light, scarcely imaginable here amid this calm autumnal setting in my native province, while the last wasps of summer are buzzing round me. My inattentive eyes wander from the pages I am leafing through to the horizon, filled now with a golden sadness by the setting sun. If nothing has changed in my museum of the past, so, too, has everything remained unaltered in this part of my town, which is becoming more and more antiquated, as its maritime activity little by little declines. The same stretches of wall, covered with the same jasmine and creepers; the same Roman-tiled roofs,[6] turning yellow with the rust of time; the same chimneys whose every outline I recognize so well against the sky at this end of an autumn day. The trees in

4. La Limoise is a property on the other side of the River Charente, where Loti used to play with his friends as a child, as related in *Le Roman d'un Enfant.*

5. The Charente rises in the Limousin, flows through Angoulême, Cognac, Saintes and Rochefort, and joins the sea in a muddy estuary. It gives its name to two *départements*, Charente and Charente-Maritime.

6. Rochefort is in an area of Roman-inspired semi-cylindrical roof tiles,

the gardens, which were already old when I began life, have not grown sensibly older since. The great elms of the ramparts, which even then were centenarian, are still there, forming a belt as magnificent as ever with their same green tops.* And when everything around has preserved itself unchanged, how difficult it is to imagine, to admit, that one is oneself nearly done with, simply because one will soon attain the number of years allotted, without mercy, to the average of existences. Heavens! to stop when you feel that nothing in you has changed, and that the same zest for adventure, for the unknown, if it still existed, would possess you still! Is it possible, alas! in the presence of this simple but unchanging scene which ought, you might think, to envelop you protectively, to impregnate you a little with its lasting faculty, in the presence of all this which perpetuates itself so easily, to have been a child for whom the world was an oyster, to have been someone *who will live* and not to be any more someone *who has lived?*

And, nevertheless, out of my short life, scattered about over the whole world, I shall have extracted something, a kind of education which does not yet suffice, but has brought already an outline of serenity. In my travels, I have seen so many places of passionate adoration, each one responding to a particular form of human agony, so many temples, mosques, cathedrals, where the same prayer has risen from the depths of the most diverse souls! These things have not only disclosed to me that cold half-proof of the existence of a God which was indicated in the philosophy class of my youth, and today is mere tedious repetition: 'the proof by the unanimous consent of mankind.' No, but something infinitely more important, namely, that such a chorus of supplications, of burning tears, imply the almost universal

---

found in the south of France (the north largely used slate). In the west the region begins on the level of Poitiers. The presence of these tiles at one stage approximately marked the furthest extent north of the *langue d'oc* speakers.

* **Of course, a council of poor silly representatives, to conform to the orders of the new social classes, has just stupidly voted for their destruction.**

confidence that this God cannot be other than a God of pity. Oh yes, I am not pretending to say in this anything that is the least bit new. I only wish to add mine to the thousands of other testimonies, because it is perhaps expected from some of my confrères. In proportion that the centuries accumulated on humanity, the savage gods which it had imagined when it first issued from its orginal darkness gradually gave place to conceptions more gentle, less crude, and, surely, less inexact. In proportion as the love of one for another, the brotherly love preached by Buddha and by Jesus, made its way into our souls, prone to more savage tendencies, the notion strengthened in us that there must be somewhere a Supreme Pity to hear our cries, and then the sanctuaries became more and more places of supplication and of tears. In the mosques of Islam, from Moghreb to Mecca, every day innumerable men, their foreheads touching the ground, appeal to the mercy of Allah. The jealous and gloomy Jehovah of the Hebrews has been effaced before the advent of Christ, and I have seen the Holy Sepulchre,[7] which is certainly the place in all the world where one hears the most confiding cries of the heart. Even at Angkor, Buddhist statues, with a smile of pardon, are seated before the four doors of the immured cella in which men, already more than a thousand years ago, felt that it was necessary to hide the terrible God of their first theogonies. More and more am I inclined to believe in the Sovereign Pity, and to open my arms to it, because I have suffered so much, under diverse skies, amid enchantments or amid horrors, and because I have seen so much suffering, seen so many tears, so many prayers. In spite of fluctuations, in spite of vicissitudes, in spite of revolts caused by narrow dogmas and exclusive formulae, one feels the existence of this Sovereign Pity affirmed more and more universally in the lofty souls who are enlightened by all the great new luminaries.*

7. Loti visited the Holy Land over three months in 1890.

*** In France, our admirable Bergson, who has overthrown determinism; in America, William James and the disciples who follow him; in India, a few**

Nowadays, it is true, we have the dregs of semi-intelligences, the partially educated, which the social regime of our time causes to rise to the surface, and which, in the name of science, rushes without understanding into the most imbecilic materialism. But, in the continued evolution, the reign of these feeble souls will mark only a negligible episode of retrogression. The Supreme Pity towards which we stretch out our despairing hands must exist, by whatever name we may call it; it must be there, capable of hearing, at the moment of separation through death, our clamour of infinite distress. For without it the Creation, to which one can no longer reasonably ascribe unawareness as an excuse, would become a cruelty too unthinkable, being odious and also cowardly.

And out of my numberless pilgrimages, futile or serious, this feeble argument, so far from being new as it is, is the only thing of value that I have been able to bring back with me.

---

wise men of Benares and Hadyar.[8] On the one side by irrefutable logic, on the other by marvellous observation, all today are coming little by little to consolidate those hopes, which our ancestors, without so much searching, were able to discover so surely and so naturally behind the symbols of intuitive religions.

8. Henri Bergson (1859–1941) believed in the liberation of mental intuitions from the idea of space and the scientific notion of time, and in the affirmation of a creative life-force. William James (1842–1910) was a founder of pragmatism and conducted important studies in analytical psychology. Benares (Varanasi) on the Ganges, long a holy city to Hindus, Buddhists and Jains, was visited by Loti in 1900. Though Hadyar is not mentioned by name in his account of India, Loti is referring to the headquarters of the Theosophical Society (founded in the United States in 1875 by Madame Blavatsky and Colonel H.S. Olcott) at Adayar (sometimes spelt Adyar) set up in a southern suburb of Madras in 1882, and which Loti visited; the reference is surprising, since Loti judged "the doctrine of these people... as puerile and vain as the little statues of the god with the elephant head, seen all long the roadside, at dawn, under the banyans and the palm trees" *(L'Inde (Sans les Anglais)* VI:I).

MICHAEL SMITHIES was born in London in 1932 and educated at the universities of Oxford, California (Berkeley) and Paris. He first came to Thailand in 1960 with the British Council, and spent the rest of his working life in Southeast Asia, teaching in universities in Hong Kong, Cambodia, Thailand, Singapore, Indonesia and Papua New Guinea, where he was foundation professor of language at the University of Technology. After five years working for the United Nations in Bangkok, Professor Smithies retired at the end of 1992, and now divides his time between Thailand and his house in France. As well as writing several volumes of short stories, he has also published numerous books and articles about English language teaching and Southeast Asian studies, and is a former series editor for Oxford University Press, honorary editor of the *Journal of the Siam Society*, and the *Journal of Oriental Studies* (Hong Kong).

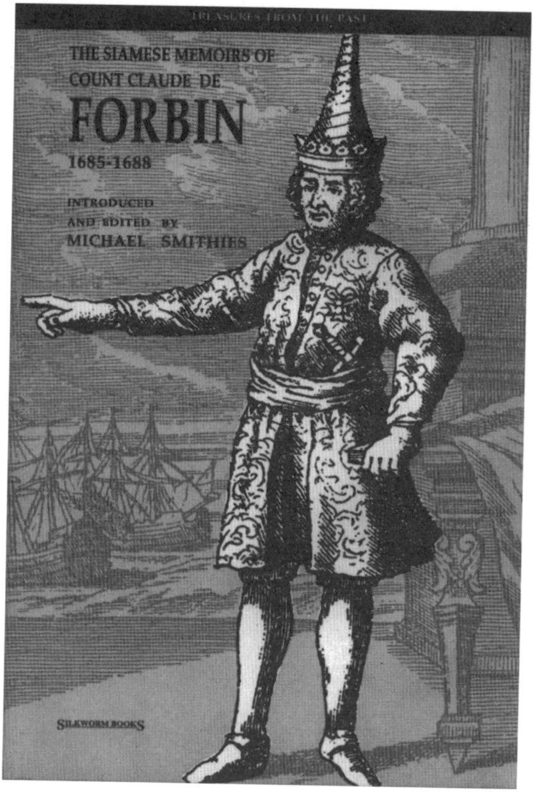

The Siamese Memoirs of Count Claude de Forbin, 1685-1688

Introduced and edited by Michael Smithies

ISBN 974-7100-30-4

1996. 190 pp, 145x210 mm, 25 b/w illus. Baht 325, US$ 10.50

Chevalier Forbin (later a count) came to Siam at the age of 29 as an aide-de-camp in the French embassy of 1685. He pleased King Narai, who made him general of the king's armies and governor of Bangkok, but he had to contend with the jealousy of the powerful Levantine minister Phaulkon. In these memoirs written at the end of his long life, he looks back on his time in Siam, tells of his experiences at the courts of Narai and Louis XIV, and describes how the French adventure in Siam ended.

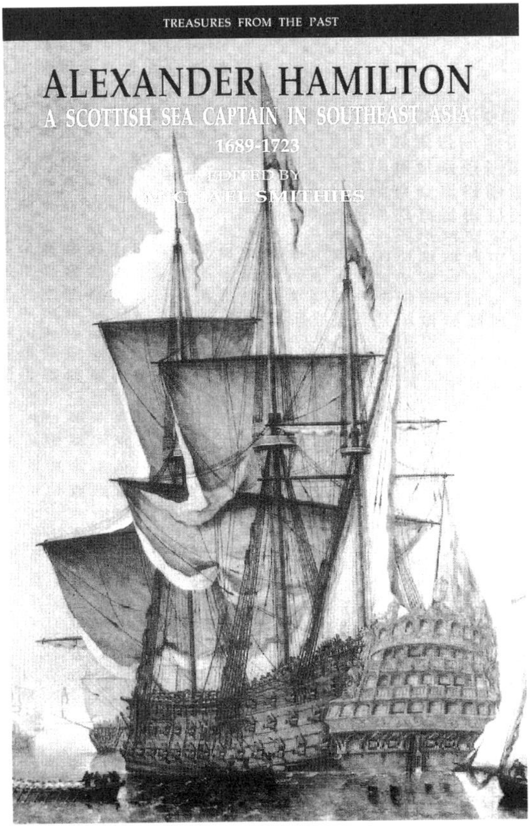

Alexander Hamilton:
A Scottish Sea Captain in Southeast Asia 1689-1723

Edited by Michael Smithies

ISBN 974-7100-45-2

1997. 206 pp, 145x210 mm, 22 b/w illus. Baht 325, US$ 10.50

Alexander Hamilton's classic text, *A New Account of the East Indies*, has only been published three times since it first appeared in Edinburgh in 1727. Its length and breadth (it covers everywhere from the Red Sea to Japan) have precluded more editions, and the most recent, the Argonaut Press limited 1930 edition, is unobtainable. Hamilton was one of the very few persons to come to Siam in the eighteenth century and leave an account of his stay. Editor Michael Smithies has taken the fourteen chapters covering Southeast Asia in Hamilton's account and provided an introduction and explanatory footnotes to the selection, with modernized spelling. This new edition of a frequently cited but rarely seen text comes with contemporary illustrations.

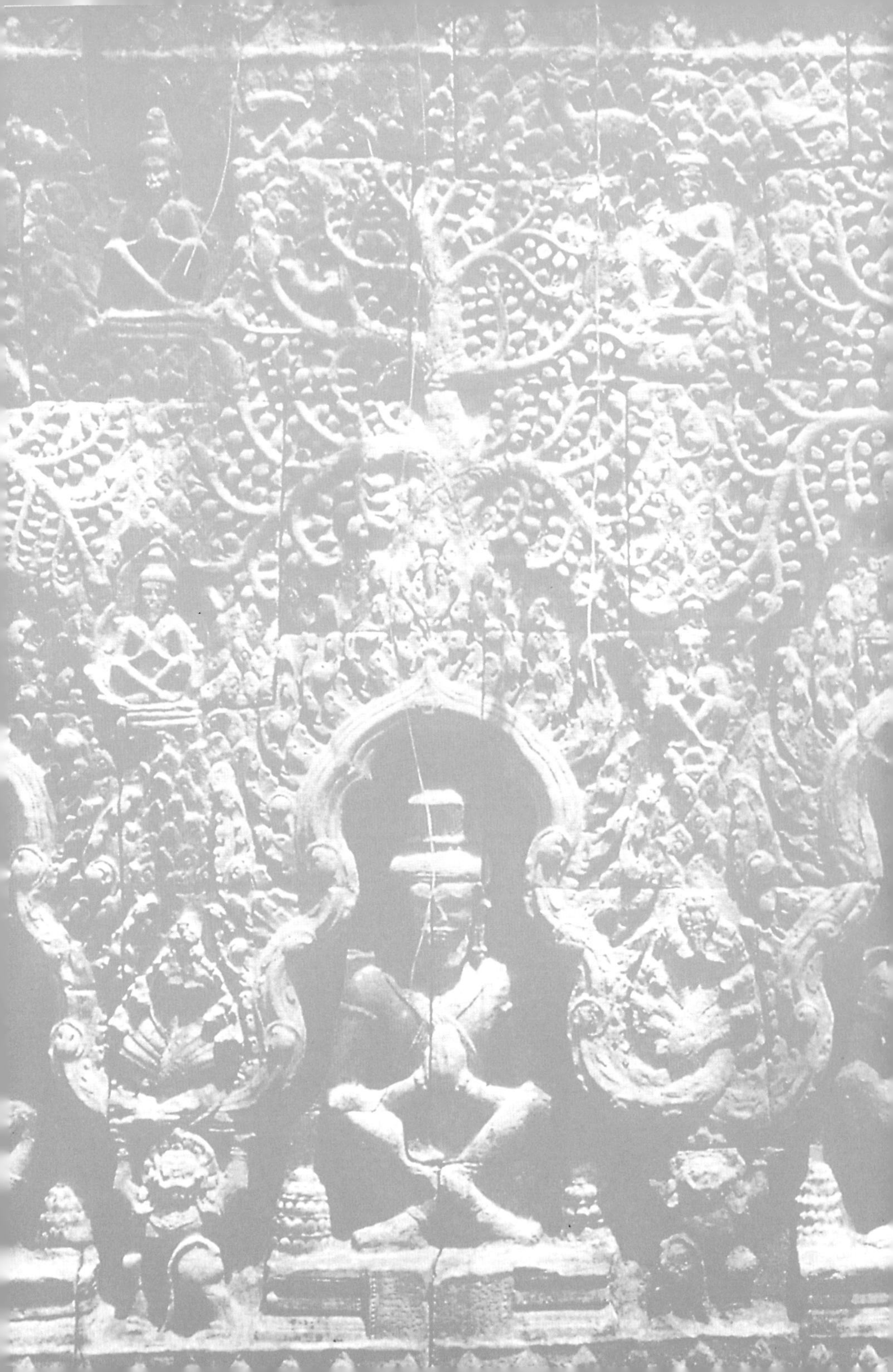